The Singing, Playing Kindergarten

The Singing, Playing Kindergarten

Daniel Udo de Haes
translated by Barbara Mees

The Singing, Playing Kindergarten

© 2015 Waldorf Early Childhood Association of North America

This book was originally published in Dutch as *de Kleuter en de Zangspelletjes*.

Translation: Barbara Mees
Cover design: Sheila Harrington
Copy editing and graphic design: Lory Widmer
Editorial consultant: Nancy Foster

ISBN: 978-1-936849-29-1

This publication was made possible by a grant from the Waldorf Curriculum Fund.

Waldorf Early Childhood Association of North America
285 Hungry Hollow Rd., Spring Valley, NY 10977
845-352-1690 / info@waldorfearlychildhood.org
www.waldorfearlychildhood.org

For a complete book catalog,
contact WECAN or visit our online store:
store.waldorfearlychildhood.org

All rights reserved. No part of this book may be reproduced in any form without the written permission of the publisher, except for brief quotations embodied in critical reviews and articles.

Contents

1 The young child's experience of rhythm — 9
2 From ritual to children's game — 13
3 Human development and singing games — 15
4 The origins of the "childhood dream" — 23
5 The imagery of singing games — 31
6 Form, movement, sound, and repetition — 39
7 Types and examples of singing games — 53
8 A healthy awakening from the "childhood dream" — 105
9 Rhythm and ritual: The possible origins of singing games — 119
10 The task of the early childhood group leader today — 131
   Music for the singing games — 141
   Notes — 157
   Recommended resources — 163
   About the author — 165

Man müsste einen Kreuzzug machen nach dem Wesen des Kleinkindes.

A crusade is needed to find the essence of the young child.

—ATTRIBUTED TO DR. ITA WEGMAN

1 The young child's experience of rhythm

While walking along the narrow sidewalk of a busy street in Rotterdam, I saw something and could scarcely believe my eyes. In the middle of all the activity—this was in the 1930s—a number of very enthusiastic schoolchildren were playing a singing game. We can hardly imagine something like it now, but even then it was remarkable. The children had formed two groups and, while clapping and stamping, they alternately sang to each other while approaching and retreating. The distance taken up by the two groups was not always appreciated by smiling passers-by. Eventually pedestrians, bikes, cargo bikes, and even slow-moving cars passed between the two groups. The children seemed hardly to notice this, and with an unfazed feeling of oneness continued their joyful clapping and stamping.

On the other side of the street a mother stood with her little girl who was about three years old. The child held a doll in her arms, but at this moment, she had no thoughts for "her baby." As if in a dream, she was completely taken in by what those big kids were doing. Paralyzed she watched, with huge eyes and a half-open mouth, completely absorbed in what was happening. The traffic didn't affect her either, but when her mother tried to pull her away, she screamed and stamped on the ground, wanting to stay. Eventually her mother picked up the protesting girl and walked on.

This unusual incident clearly shows the difference in the relationship between play and rhythm for a schoolchild and a toddler. The schoolchildren on the street, led by a few ten-to-twelve-year-olds, lost themselves completely in the strictly-formed rhythm of the game; the toddler, also lost in the rhythmic happenings, watched motionless but let out completely un-rhythmical, emotional screams and struggled terribly when disturbed.

For a schoolchild, active rhythm is a necessity of life. If rhythm cannot be expressed, in school or artistically, the child cannot be truly healthy and flourish. The number of psychologically disturbed people, including adults, who received an unrhythmical and therefore unimaginative, one-sided education is countless. The example of this group of schoolchildren in Rotterdam clearly shows how strongly a child of this age lives in active rhythm. We can therefore imagine what would be destroyed in the child's development if this primary necessity of life were withheld—something that unfortunately happens all too often. Great efforts will be needed if this process is to change.

As we saw in the streets of Rotterdam, the toddler lives in a completely different rhythmic element. How unnatural would it have been if the little girl on the sidewalk, completely absorbed in what the older children were doing, had tried to join the game! She saw the rhythmic game that touched her innermost being and in which she lost herself, but actively joining would have been impossible. Inwardly she was one with them, outwardly paralyzed, dreamily captivated by the rhythm, but not yet able to join in. If we were to expect her to do so, or to try to teach her, however gradually and lovingly, it would be at the expense of her inner rhythmic experience and ultimately her soul life. Much of her cosmic soul would then lose the possibility to evolve.

The kindergarten years, which come between these two stages of toddlerhood and school readiness, also come in between them rhythmically. In other words, something from both sides lives in the kindergarten-age child. The toddler in him has a dreaming experience of rhythm; as he grows towards being a schoolchild, he is given the possibility to join in step by step. However, as long as he is a kindergartner, this ability to play rhythmically is very different from that of a schoolchild. He has not yet reached the level of energetic determination that he will have at that age, and still has the dreaming character of a toddler, however cheerful his rhythmical movements are. If we were to expect active and awake rhythmic games meant for the schoolchild from him, we would make him skip an important rhythmical development phase, with all the negative consequences that that would bring.

Nowadays we see that the active rhythmic experience, so needed by the schoolchild, is withheld almost everywhere. Furthermore, it is often forced onto the children in the kindergarten, who could thus be seriously damaged in their development. Everything is accelerated and people think that the children will benefit from this. If we're not careful, we may come to a point where we will teach infants to thrash about rhythmically! We know and feel that this is utter nonsense, but not everyone knows that pushing the rhythmical development of a child can have extremely negative consequences.

In his book *The Education of the Child*,[1] Rudolf Steiner discusses the transition from toddler to kindergartner and likens it to taking a step out of the cosmic origin world into life on earth. In the context of rhythm and singing games, we should see this step as moving from the still dreaming, cosmic, rhythmic experience of the toddler to the strong, active, rhythmic play of the school child—a development that extends throughout the kindergarten years. All the steps taken by the still-cosmic toddler into the next life phase are steps taken out of the previous soul environment and into the earthly world. The child crosses the threshold between the cosmic and earthly worlds. In the case of rhythmic awareness, the threshold is wide and the child needs all of the kindergarten years to cross it.

A mixed-age kindergarten consists of children between the toddler phase and the beginning of school. In other words, all phases and levels of this wide threshold are present. Our subtle but comprehensive task is to give every child what he or she needs, but at the same time guard them all against hurriedly taking the step into active rhythm, especially when it comes to singing games. In our Rotterdam adventure, all the children who were playing were the right age for the game, while the little girl watching was not. In kindergarten, some children are ready, in differing degrees. This is something I clearly saw while leading a group of kindergartners. Often I played singing games with the older children while my helper did something different with the smaller ones: cutting, pasting, working with beeswax.

Each group leader must decide for herself how to bridge this gap. However, since these games are often played in the kindergarten environment, we don't want to deny the fact that they can bring much good, especially when led well. In the next chapters we will delve further into the relationship of the kindergarten years and these games.

2 | From ritual to children's game

We cannot be sure of the historical origins of the first singing games, but the fact that these games were such a natural part of the life of schoolchildren, as well as the deep wisdom and widespread use of them, leads us to believe that they may stem from ritual or cultic sources. It would not surprise me to find that they stem from ancient religions, where rhythmical round dances were practiced. For prehistoric human beings, rhythm played an important role, especially in rituals, as they lived more in their limbs than in thinking. (Chapter Nine will further explore this subject.) It could be that with the development of logical thinking, rhythmic-religious ritual elements were gradually taken over by young people, and finally by children—whereby the structured character of the ritual changed into that of a game.

I participated in these well-known singing games when I was a schoolchild, around 1908, and experienced how children learned the games quite naturally from each other. The younger ones grew up with them, first watching and gradually joining in; children who became too old just stopped doing them. The games survived and were played by neighborhood friends in quiet corners of squares where there was hardly any traffic, or on lawns between the houses. This declined due to the growing amount of traffic and changes in people's lives. The event in Rotterdam can be seen as unusual considering the date and the city location with all its traffic.

At this time kindergartens started to evolve, and singing games were increasingly used in these groups. Unfortunately, the games were lost to older schoolchildren not only because of the increase in traffic but because schoolwork became more and more intellectual.

We should be grateful to kindergarten group leaders that the old singing games have not been lost completely, but we have seen how important it is to use the games wisely. There are more stumbling blocks for a young child than rhythm alone. These games reveal secrets of the character of school-children in various ways. We therefore need to adjust the games to the needs of kindergartners. When the games ask for the children to walk in a long line, or to choose another child, or make up and show a movement, we will have to jump in and help the little ones to prevent them from feeling lost or, even worse, from showing off. If they start showing off, they lose their innocence and bypass the "dream stage" that is still so much part of their life. We will come back to these matters in a later chapter.

3 | Human development and singing games

One could see how circle dances may have evolved: from ritual dances for adults (as we imagine them to have been used), to games for schoolchildren, and in turn, "naturally" developing into games for kindergartners. If we really see this development as "natural," then the next step would be to toddlers. Don't forget, however, that such developments always have their lows and highs. If this were not the case, we would see it evolving further to babies and then. . . ? This development is unthinkable without a change in direction.

In our opinion there seems to be a strong relationship between this change in direction and a much larger change that has been going on in the development of mankind. This is happening through the devaluation and materialization of man's inner spirit that is reaching its lowest point, from which lost soul content must be found again. Human beings are longing to rediscover their humanity. Human consciousness, which has become rigidified by the intellect, can now be enlivened and take on new forms.

In ancient times, initiates in the mysteries led people inwardly through ceremonies, myths, and legends. When these leaders withdrew, their position was only partly taken over by the church. The more "cosmic" knowledge of the initiates was not adopted, with the result that the consciousness of humanity became much more rational and intellectualism, while materialism had the chance to spread widely. But there was a deeper meaning behind the withdrawal of the initiates. When they were no longer led, human beings were given the chance to become spiritually independent. By becoming spiritually independent, they became more and more aware of the fact that their deeper, inner life had been lost. Through this consciousness, and because of this new independence, a search for the lost inner meaning began.

We can now follow our own lead in our search for inner meaning, but only if we want to. A spiritual science that stems from the same deep sources and cosmic guidance as the early mysteries now has a completely new character, which leaves human beings in newly-acquired independence. Thus it can school us in discovering and redeveloping our own deeper humanity.

When considering the young child, we believe that the awakened adult consciousness could free the child within. We are seeing a growing necessity to safeguard and guide that inner part of a child that is in danger of perishing in our modern world: the small measure of cosmic soul life still in him. And when that child carries this small seed through his life and allows it to flourish as he gets older, we hope that it will create a foundation for a new future, at first only for those searching but later for more widespread circles.

In *The Education of the Child,*[2] Rudolf Steiner describes how the human spiritual being receives a threefold dwelling place on earth. Aside from the physical body, it also has an "etheric" shell, the "etheric body" or "life body." This body carries life, growth, and formative powers as well as the rhythmical element of our being. The third sheath is our "astral" or "consciousness body," in which cosmic forces work and all soul functions have their foundations. That which we call the birth of a child is actually only the birth of the physical body. The life, or etheric, body is born with the change of teeth and announces that the child is ready for the start of formal education. The astral body presents itself in adolescence as a need for independence. This is when puberty sets in. Our soul body itself, also called the "I," formed in ancient times, enters the physical body around our twenty-first year (although nowadays sometimes earlier) and is experienced as a more pronounced consciousness; in other words, the I is "born."

Saying that the etheric body is born when a child begins the change of teeth does not mean that it is not already active. The opposite is true. The etheric body is active "behind the scenes" in the formation of the organs and in the unparalleled physical growth of the first years of life. The first tooth that falls out gives the sign that the organs have been completed so that the etheric body can come forward and start its work. Rhythmical awareness, new interests and thoughts about the outside world, and the desire to learn through new activities and possibilities show that the etheric body has arrived.

Thus, to promote a healthy development of the child, we are encouraged to wait to introduce such elements (including active rhythm) until the first teeth are changed. We should be careful not to be tempted by circumstances and requests by kindergartners to be awakened from their "dream" and brought to "active" rhythm. This being said, however, we should consider each child individually. If certain children are very precocious in their development, yearn for something new, and no longer respond to activities fitting their age, it will be difficult to divert their attention. We cannot correct such a development by force, however much we would like to. In terms of rhythmical development it will be best to go along with such a child's wishes until it is possible to direct the course back to healthier channels, without being misled by the eagerness of the child. The forbidden fruit tasted good for both Adam and Eve! We must be aware that in their eagerness, these children are skipping a step in their development. Their precociousness, their will to grasp the external part of life, means that they are neglecting to connect their inner being with earthly life. Through this rift much of their deeper soul content will stay "unborn." It will pine away and may cast a shadow on the rest of their life.

A great deal of responsibility and insight is demanded from us when dealing with a whole group of children in the kindergarten who have already come into contact with these strong rhythmic games. If even part of the group has tasted the forbidden fruit, it will not be easy to guide them back, however gradually. And if forced, we risk creating tensions that could hurt the group beyond measure. Still, as mentioned before, we can safeguard new children coming into kindergarten from the still-too-strong rhythm by asking our helper to do something else with them, possibly together with some of the "less rhythmic" little ones. Further, when we do let these little ones carefully participate in the games, it is of the utmost importance that we let them participate freely, without asking for rhythmic clapping and stamping. In this way, slowly but steadily, the whole group will regain its level of health.

Modern society generally pulls young children out of their dream world too soon not only through the things around them (radio, television, modern technology, traffic) but also through the way adults and older children live modern life. Alarm clocks go off everywhere! We must do our best to protect the inner development of the child from this danger. By doing this you are not "spoiling" the children, much as infants are not "spoiled" when given milk (preferably breast milk), instead of scrambled eggs, finely ground meat, or clear soup because we think that this will give them more nutrition and they should get used to it. Everyone understands that if we were to give newborns solid foods their system would become completely unbalanced. But not everyone understands how harmful it is for a child's spiritual constitution if it is given spiritual food that accelerates movement to the next life phase. It is only through compassion for the inner development of children that we will be able to give them experiences that fit where they are in life. If we give them nutrients that will accelerate their growth we will rob them of deeper soul content. The pedagogical foundations brought by Rudolf Steiner are largely made up of an exact account of what is needed and of what one should be careful of in each phase of childhood.

When observing how young people develop with more and more haste, we often hear people say, "He is a child of his time!" But is this true? Shouldn't we say, "*We* are adults of our time"? Doesn't that mean, much more so than before, that we should acquire a consciousness for these new developments? The growth of awareness for the danger of something such as traffic is apparent, but as modern people we must understand that exposing children's inner being to these dangers is even worse. Destiny has put their future in our care and it is up to us to guide them through the threats that may stand in the way of a healthy life.

In the rest of this book we will consider and attempt to answer the questions of why accelerating development is so harmful, what happens when the right soul food is given, and how we can do this, especially when looking at singing games.

We would like to avoid sticking "passive" or "active" labels on the various rhythmic experiences of the toddler, kindergartner, and schoolchild. The sleeping rhythmic experience of the toddler is, as seen on the sidewalk in Rotterdam, outwardly "passive," but the inner self may be very lively and active. Instead of inactive, we could speak of a "dream rhythm." Dreams, without becoming reality, can be very lively. Then, to distinguish between the inwardly active "dream rhythm" of the toddler, we should not see the rhythm of the school child as "active" but rather as "deed rhythm." The kindergartner lives in the transition between the toddler's "dream rhythm" and the "deed rhythm" of the schoolchild.

The question is not whether rhythm should play a part in the kindergarten group, but rather how and to what degree, considering all the phases of transition, and how we should act and lead the group. The group should never arrive at the full active rhythm of a schoolchild, but we should be careful not to completely avoid rhythm, however dreamy the youngest member of the group is. It is up to the leader to find her subtle way around all the obstacles so that she can lead each child individually, as well as the group as a whole, down the rhythmic road that the kindergartner must take.

For the youngest children, the rhythms of the cosmos and of their own families and homes form the foundation, and remain so throughout kindergarten. Children experience life's rhythms through the changes from day to night and season to season, and through life at home in general. For example, Father leaves for work in the morning, comes home again in the evening, and plays with the child by bouncing her rhythmically on his knees. An older sister plays "Row, row, row your boat" with her. From birth, rhythm is passed on to the infant by the mother through the alternation between waking and sleeping, nursing and changing. Children who do not receive this primitive rhythm in their first months and years can be seriously hurt and disadvantaged in their will system, and suffer detrimental consequences both physically and mentally.

All people experience cosmic and life rhythms. But the young child, and especially the infant, experiences them even more—although more out of instinct than consciously. The different relationships to forms of rhythm are present and are important in pre-school and kindergarten groups. Cosmic rhythms (night and day, the seasons) are automatic, but motherly care, and the daily rhythm of parents or siblings, should be reflected by the group leader as much as possible during the day. If the leaders can create a balanced environment, full of imagination and geared to the various ages of the children, we can expect that the children will develop their own healthy human rhythm that will become "deed rhythm," ready for school and continuing to grow during the rest of their lives.

Silently present through all the phases of development described above is the will to imitate everything that a child sees in other children and adults. For adults this brings responsibility. A child will imitate *everything*, that which is seen or unseen, good or bad. Therefore it is of the utmost importance that the adult set a good example.

Among infants, imitation takes place subconsciously. Everything that happens around them is internalized and only becomes visible much later. However, it forms the basis of all aspects of their development. Even after the baby years, this subconscious imitation continues to be important. The toddler in the streets of Rotterdam internalized the strong rhythm of the schoolchildren without moving an inch; it would stay dormant until she was ready to show it through her own deed rhythm when a schoolchild.

As with this young girl, the inner, dormant imitation plays an important role in every kindergarten group, not just for the children but also for the leader. Although these processes are concealed from us, it is important that we as adults get a feel for them and try to see the formative meaning they have for the children.

In order to see the line of development of rhythm in early childhood, we should find songs and later singing games that can be used from cradle to grade school to accompany children in their development. The earliest songs should be soft lullabies that have a dreaming rhythm as well as melodic character. Such songs can also be sung with toddlers while on our knee, and with kindergartners we can slowly add the game element without being too "awake," as in "White swans and black swans" (see Chapter Seven). Songs with a somewhat more awake rhythm—we'd rather not speak of "more joyful," as the dreaming rhythm is joyful in its own way—can be used for slightly older kindergartners, such as "Have you ever heard of the seven leap" or "Come show me your feet (The Washerwomen)." Finally, we can venture upon songs that have challenging fourths and strongly accented rhythms. We should envelop them with much care to soften the hard, almost sharp edges, even for the older kindergartners. In spite of this, these singing games have such valuable content that playing them is definitely worthwhile.

Of course, it goes without saying that the nature of the rhythm in the singing game depends on the way it is presented by the group leader. One and the same game can be presented with a more cosmic or earthly orientation, depending on the occasion or on the age of the children. But even so, some games are better for the one than for the other and it is important that we develop a consciousness for the various rhythmic forms in order to be able to use them in the various kindergarten age groups. To start with, it is important that we try to put aside our own active adult "deed rhythm" so that we can understand the still-dreaming rhythm of the kindergartner.

Another important point is the mood created through the musical tones used. Almost all folksongs are written in the "normal" diatonic scale—mostly in major keys, a few in minor—while the kindergartner, and even the schoolchild until the ninth year, should actually not have to conform to these elements. However, the melodies of these old songs are often so dreamy that the major or minor mode is not too apparent, or they can be sung in such a way that this element becomes less important. They leave the children in their dreamy state.

There is one scale that lingers in the cosmic element, playing an important role in early music, and that can now again become of importance through its floating, dreaming character: the pentatonic scale G-A-B-D-E. This scale, which is already being used in anthroposophical circles in new kindergarten songs and singing games, should be studied separately.[3] Suffice it to say that this scale is the basis for melodies most favorable, suitable, and beautiful for the "dream rhythm" of the small child.

The above considerations about the still-cosmic disposition of toddlers and kindergarten-age children and their "childhood dream" could lead to misperceptions. We could have the impression that these children are far-off beings who have not yet woken up, and in the usual sense of the word are "dreamers" instead of "dreamy." It should be obvious that neither is the case. Everyone knows how lively and spontaneous the still-so-changeable moods of young children may be in their outward expression: skipping or jumping with pleasure, crying in sadness or screaming in rage. Still, everything arises from an inner "dream-like" state. As soon as a conscious wakefulness is desired from young children, they will automatically withdraw and turn away.

The inner "dream-like" state is so crucial to kindergarten-age children's development that we can only understand them if we find a connection with the hidden essence of this "early childhood dreaminess," which is of such importance in their daily life.

4 The origins of the "childhood dream"

Where can we find the origins of the "childhood dream"? In order to answer this question, we would like to use another example taken from daily life.

In a quiet street in Zeist I once saw a small boy, probably three years old, squatting beside a puddle left in the street after the last rain shower. With complete concentration, the boy moved his hand through the water very slowly. It was obvious that nothing else existed for him at that moment other than the water in that puddle. Being absorbed in what we call the "ordinary" things of life is so typical for a young child, especially a toddler. Kindergarten-age children can also have these kinds of experiences, even though they have a livelier fantasy life. It is important that we give them enough time and peace to internalize these moments, which show them their special path from the cosmos to earthly life. Such moments can only be understood if we put ourselves in the shoes of young children and try to experience everything as if for the first time.

Try to remember that it was only a short while ago, before birth, that this child was in a completely different world: the pre-birth soul world. Though it cannot be proven, more and more people feel that man's soul does not originate either from nothing or from matter.[4] For many, this means that the soul is born out of the spirit and that this spirit will continue its life even after the body has died. Consequently there should also be a development before birth that influences the soul's particular traits and possibilities.

The thought of a life before birth that gives deeper meaning to many otherwise inexplicable events can help us come closer to the essence of the "childhood dream." We can sometimes feel something of the pre-birth cosmic soul world in the facial expression of a child. Especially when young children observe something in complete silent concentration, we can sometimes see in their eyes that they are reminded of something in the concealed past of the soul. It seems as if we are watching a "life in two worlds." For example, when a toddler is captivated by a group of older children playing a singing game, we might feel something of the life of the soul in the spiritual world where it lived among the angels. We feel how the child's soul experienced the "weaving-sounding," almost "spiritually eurythmic" life and creative work of the angels, how he observed and lived among the "circles of angels." It is not for nothing that one Dutch lullaby contains the words "In heaven there is a dance. . . There the little virgins dance" (i.e. all the angels and all the chaste souls). The child sees the children "dancing" as the virgins in his memory, concealed but still very much alive in his soul. No wonder the little girl on the sidewalk, in the anecdote related earlier, screamed when she had to leave this heavenly spectacle on earth.

Experiences such as these are important for the rest of a child's life. Children experience the union of heaven and earth, of the spiritual and the earthly worlds, as a sense of a "physical" soul world. We hope that they may then find the possibility to carry as much soul content as possible across the threshold to earth.

We would now like to look more closely at the little boy beside the puddle mentioned at the beginning of this chapter. We have already spoken about our "life body," that which carries life, growth, and formative powers. This life, or etheric, body, which continually feeds us refreshing health, allows the soul to receive a flow of energy and life forces from the "lake" of spiritual forces in which it resides. Even when on earth, these etheric forces still replenish the young child—he still feels very close to the bank of the "lake of etheric forces." So now he sees a puddle of rainwater on the earth. Couldn't it be possible that while looking at the rainwater, or shall we say "heavenly fluid," he is reminded of this lake? Here we see an encounter between heaven and earth that is so inconceivably intense for the child that his soul can't get enough of it; his dreaming mode of consciousness makes it all the more powerful. In tangible reality the boy sees that his spirit has come down into his physical body.

In this example, much as with the little girl on the sidewalk, we see the "dreaming recognition" of the spirit in the earthly world. Young children continually experience this recognition, making their entire earthly surroundings an "open secret," as Goethe put it.

Water not only symbolizes flowing cosmic etheric powers; it is also the most important bearer of all life processes in nature, as well as in our own bodies. It is the "life fluid" of the earth and of our bodies; for example, in our blood, water bears the blood cells and other elements. Water also behaves in a unique way: time and time again it rises to the cosmos only to return filled with heavenly forces with which to enrich the earth. Likewise the human soul repeatedly returns to the spiritual world and comes back for a new earthly life: "The human soul, how like the water," wrote Goethe. Thus we can liken a young child to a large raindrop. She has just come into her earthly form from the cosmos and still carries the heavenly gift that can replenish many an earthly person.

Each and every young child loves to play with water, most likely because of an inner kindred feeling with and a dreaming recognition of this miraculous "earthly life fluid" with all its unsolved mysteries. What we adults might see as making a terrible mess is for children a return to the pre-birth "heavenly lake" that gives their souls new strength and is of the utmost importance for their further development. The little boy with his hands in the puddle saw and felt part of his pre-birth life in heaven and in this "earthly lake" saw something of the larger "heavenly lake" whose strength will live on in him throughout his earthly life.

This is what the earliest years are all about: recognizing these heavenly gifts on earth and being able to internalize them in order to carry them along in earthly life. We need to learn to see how the healthy child who is not yet made superficial by the modern world is engulfed by the experiences of both worlds. Whereas we adults only see "ordinary" things and miss the sheer magnitude of these experiences, the child sees much more.

On the one hand bound to earth by the senses, on the other hand lingering in the pre-birth spiritual world, the soul of the young child leads a twofold life that can be spiritually compared to the amphibious phase. The special bond that the child feels with water emphasizes the amphibious character of this life phase.

Meanwhile, we must understand that it is particularly toddlers and kindergarten-age children, not infants, who have this spiritually amphibious character. Amphibians can live out of the water. Infants, though they have left the physical amniotic fluid that carried them, continue to be borne by the pre-birth cosmic soul environment. The impressions made on their senses by the new world work deeply into their souls, but almost all *come to them*. These impressions can hardly be experienced inwardly; they form the children's surroundings. Think back to the previously described rhythm of day and night and motherly care, which bear infants in a deep, dreaming experience. There is very little that the infants actually observe, however. Everything happens *to* them. In contrast, not only because they can do more physically but also out of their inner being, toddlers are completely wrapped up in their new environment. This intrigues them so much that they seem to be "all sense organ." If we stay with the example of water, we see that an infant can only really experience it, seeing, hearing, and feeling it, while being washed. Somewhat later, when he is put in his bath, we see him splash about, which shows a new type of experience. But a toddler goes to a puddle that he has found *himself,* and stirs the water with his own hand. The infant "is surrounded by his surroundings"; the toddler is not only surrounded by but also experiences his surroundings. He experiences life in two worlds, something that the kindergarten-age child continues to do but in a slightly different way.

If we continue to use the amphibian image, we can think of a frog, for instance, and we can then compare the infant to a tadpole. Before birth, the soul lived in the spirit fully and was, like a tadpole, completely in its element, in water. Infants, who also receive impressions from the surroundings (and in a few instances, can already experience tiny things themselves) still live mostly like tadpoles—that is, their cosmic environment still primarily carries them.

It is only after children have had the first "no" phase, with their first acts of disobedience towards parental authority, and are almost at the point of saying "I," that the first steps towards independence—shall we say, "steps on dry land"—can be taken. They can now perceive their surroundings from the (spiritual) water world as well as from the earthly world, and can experience this transition through their newly acquired independence. Now the child has become a true amphibian, like the frog who lives on dry earth as well as being able to dive back into the water, thus keeping his skin "wet" in order to stay healthy.

Only toddlers and kindergarten-age children live in this way; infants hardly do at all, and schoolchildren, especially the older ones, don't live like this *any more*. But the phenomenon is most evident, of course, in those children who are cosmically oriented. In their daily lives, these children live in the earthly world as well as lingering in their spiritual past. Almost every earthly impression is experienced from an earthly viewpoint as well as spiritually. In Roman mythology the god Janus had two faces, because he could look ahead into the future of humanity and at the same time look back into the spiritual past. This is what young children do, especially those who are cosmically inclined. They see a future world of sense-perceptions ahead and at the same time the spiritual "background" of everything that has been behind. (The first month of the year, January, is also named after Janus. This month takes us from the old into the new year. It is the month with "two faces.")

One could say that each human child carries a twofold view toward the earthly future and the spiritual past that was once present in all humanity. Children live in the mystery of the meeting of these two worlds: of the spirit and of the senses, heaven and earth, inward and outward. When observing them, we will be able to see this more and more clearly, which can become a wonderful adventure.

We can find the Janus-experience in its most primitive form in the story of Adam and Eve being forced to leave paradise, or descend from cosmic to earthly life. This primeval drama takes place in each human being in the descent from the cosmos to earth, however little one can remember of it in later life. If we want to fully understand the importance of this life phase that each of us has gone through but has forgotten, and how essential it is for the rest of earthly life, we will once more have to place ourselves in the shoes of the child.

For young children it is an exciting adventure to discover cosmic content in the things around them and in their experiences. This is what absorbs them in early childhood and makes it possible for them to introduce the cosmic self into earthly life—not consciously, but rather in the dreaming subconscious. When what was hidden in the soul has fulfilled its role of laying a foundation for later life and growth, it can come to the surface in a "ripening" process. Thus, much that is already strongly connected to the value of our life slumbers deep in our souls, only to awaken through certain experiences or moments of turning inward where it can at last perform its actual task.[5]

By now it should be clear that the question of whether the soul will go through life with a wealth of inner resources and possibilities or in spiritual poverty has everything to do with how the soul has lived through the early years and to what degree it has been able to connect these spiritual resources to earthly life.

Nowadays, more than ever, the future of young children lies in the hands of adults. The question is whether adults can provide a healthy "home" for these souls, resisting the pace of today's sped-up society, which may encourage giving children meaningless stories, unsuitable pictures and toys, and a technical environment with too much television and radio. Such practices pull children down to earth much too quickly.

In many ways these first years are of even more importance for those children who are slower in development, but they are also important for those who are gifted. The former need extra guidance and help in incarnating. For the latter it would be good to have a long time for the "childhood dream" or an "amphibious phase" so that their vast soul content can settle into the physical body. If this time is not given these children's gifts may not surface, which sometimes results in them becoming eccentric and not finding their place in life.

Although we are helped and led by a higher power, it is not for nothing that humanity achieved independence, however inadequately. Within our independence we human beings must try to find our own way to see and accept the offered help. This is important not only for ourselves and others but especially for children. We cannot survive without the spiritual world, but the spiritual world cannot function without us either. It needs us to achieve its goals on earth. When we see what we have to achieve for the young child, the help of the spiritual world is essential. It is our task to accompany children in their search for the entrance to this world and to give them as much leadership as possible. In order to be able to help them cross the threshold from the spiritual world to earthly life, we will have to fully understand how they live in the cosmos and on earth at the same time, since they will recognize and relive their cosmic side in everything that surrounds them. That which comes with the child and wants to find its way on earth must be led in these first years by someone who sees and understands both of these worlds.

This is, of course, as important at home as in the nursery or kindergarten. At home, children cannot always mess with water the way they can at school. In general, playing with clay and painting are not done very often at home and there is little time to tell fairy tales. Parents know that this is done at school and thus this part of the child's life is entrusted to others. However, it should be obvious that nothing can be a substitute for the home. The father and the mother continue to be important, and it is essential that they also understand what is happening in their child so that they can do their part. It is in the home that the foundations are laid, and only when they are laid properly can early childhood educators erect the walls on these foundations. Thus a bridge is built between the spiritual and earthly worlds.

5 | The imagery of singing games

The intensity with which toddlers and kindergartners experience their environment, whether in play or while listening to a fairy tale, is not obvious. The children do not sit quietly, at least not visibly. But when we observe more closely, we can feel that they do experience such activities intensely, but while in movement. Their abandonment in play *with* but also *in* movement can both be just as intense. We often see that movement is essential for a full experience: a toddler must stir the water with her hand or scoop sand in a bucket only to let it flow out again in order to connect with this element; a kindergartner becomes a "chauffeur" or "builder" and experiences these roles through play.

But how about the singing games that the children in the kindergarten have never played and would never play if they were not taught? Here is something completely new!

We have already seen that in today's kindergartens singing games have become an essential element and that they bring something new and healthy, fitting for this age group. What can a child or a group of children experience during these singing games?

The answer to this question will come if we think of where the child lived only a short while ago: in the cosmic world, surrounded by higher beings who inhabit an even higher world. When we think of how the child's soul lived among the hosts of angels, we may understand how a singing game, played dreamily, will allow the child to re-live this phase through movement—no less intensely nor less deeply than when listening quietly to a fairy tale.

There are both differences and similarities between singing games and fairy tales. The singing game addresses the element of movement more directly than the fairy tale, while the fairy tale addresses the child's hidden etheric will system. The game is active but also tranquil; the fairy tale is tranquil but also active.

Aside from movement, and the previously discussed element of rhythm, singing games also possess the element of imagery. This imagery, although partly the same as in fairy tales, works differently because of the songs' melody and rhythm. For example, the "white swans and black swans" that "sail with us to England" could easily be part of a fairy tale. This will be discussed in more detail later in this book.

The imagery that singing games present is of a completely different character, inexpressible in words. These are the images that are created: a circle, a line, walking (in a circle, and in a line or procession), dividing into two groups, singing and responding to each other. The imagery created through play and movement is much stronger than the spoken word of the fairy tales, and because it is physical it addresses the element of will in the child.

Let us now look at the special role that the *circle* plays. Many games are played in a circle. It is understandable that this form is very important for many children. The harmonious, binding element of this form speaks to us all, but it can present problems for young children. For toddlers it is almost impossible to sit in a circle. At this age, the child is not yet socially aware and shouldn't, or even can't, be expected to be social. A toddler has not yet experienced his "I" and the first formations of this consciousness belong in the intimacy of the home, to the "domestic circle." This age group needs this intimacy. Nowadays, because the intimacy of the home is increasingly threatened, pre-schools and kindergartens are being asked more and more often to take over and expand their role. It is an even greater task for us to make sure that neither we nor our surroundings ask too much from the child socially, so as not to crush the slumbering origins from which true social awareness has yet to grow. If the circle element is used with tact and flexibility, it will be a favorable element within any early childhood setting.

This is especially true for the new children just joining the kindergarten group. A child who is new will not only feel disoriented in the "play circle" but also in the "circle" of the entire kindergarten. This disorientation can cause a small inner shock for some young children. If we are aware of this, we will also be able to understand that when certain children do not react or seem to pull back into their shells, this is not a return to the "childhood dream." The confrontation with new impulses can "wake them up" subconsciously, something that is quite sad as they still need the nourishment that comes out of the "between-two-worlds dream."

In order to take care of the less favorable aspects of the "new atmosphere" and turn them into positive traits, it is important that newcomers feel at home in their new environment as quickly as possible. It is the group leader's task to envelop them in the right amount of warmth and harmony but also to observe each child's development. While one child will look for a replacement for the now "lost" mother, another may not be able to trust immediately and will need to take the first steps of this enormous transition in silence.

The same two possibilities appear in the new "domestic circle." One child can experience a positive impulse when seeing this new circle portrayed in the play circle, a circle that would very much like to include her. For another child, who finds all these new impulses hard to digest, the play circle is still too much and just the sight of it can be frightening. It is better to let this child play or look at a picture book somewhere else in the room, preferably together with a few other children. The unfavorable waking-up element of all these new impulses will thus be minimized, leaving the child to become acquainted with them slowly. If children have been given enough time to assimilate these impulses in silence, they will usually carefully join the play circle when they are ready.

Once they have joined the circle, the embracing role of the kindergarten, the "new domestic circle," will be strengthened and deepened through the circle play. We then hope that such children will have made the transition from "own mother" to "new mother," from trusted home to new home without harm and will have used it to their advantage, allowing new possibilities to arise.

Knowing what problems and pitfalls circle play can have for the children, what can possibly be the positive side to these games? Once the inner shock has passed and the children have been able to relax and join the circle element, we notice that they begin to experience a deep "recollection." Weren't they, not so very long ago, together with many others in the cosmic world? And isn't this cosmic soul community of the child, although much smaller, also present in the kindergarten? The first steps to a still-dreaming social awareness are taken; the feeling of a human cosmic soul community, the "human circle," can have its first "dreaming birth" on earth. In this way the rudiments of human nature can take on the dreaming form needed for further development in young human beings.

The children also experience a deeper, subconscious recollection of their previous life. In the cosmic world their souls lived with other human souls but, as we discussed before, were also accompanied by higher cosmic beings. Where previously the elements of song and movement became abandonment in movement—we could say abandonment to the "hymns" of higher beings—there is now the "circle" of the human soul surrounded and protected by the angels. The children's souls lived, and still live, surrounded by the cosmic protection of the angels, much more so than with us adults. Our dream consciousness, where all this takes place, is much weaker than that of the child; we cannot consciously remember anything of these higher worlds. Things were very different a long time ago. In the Bible and in myths and legends, as well as in today's spiritual science, angels are mentioned and described. Early humanity knew about angelic beings, whom they called "gods" or "goddesses" and with whom they had a definite connection.

The dream consciousness of the child is much more connected with early humanity than is the adult's. We can read about the angelic world and can therefore know a lot about it, but we can hardly experience it anymore. Young children *know* nothing about this world, except the little that they have been told, but in their dream consciousness it plays a very important role. The angelic world still lives in the deepest part of their souls and they feel protected.

Children will experience dreaming recognition in what they see and do. Being carried by the spirit of the kindergarten group and especially the warmth of the leader plays an important role. Through this protective haven, the "circle element" that comes from higher beings can manifest itself on earth.

Finding an entrance to earthly life through the physical form in childhood is important not only for the present moment but also for the rest of a human being's life. By taking on the human form, soul content can slowly start its work in the development of the children. In adulthood, people can look back on their early years and those profound experiences and ask themselves: Where did that come from? And while searching, they could ask themselves further questions and thus experience their inner development in the relationship between the cosmic and earthly worlds. What children experienced dreamily can become the link between these two worlds in adulthood, in a more conscious way and with a look towards the future. In this way, through their own free will, they can try to connect with the world of their first dreaming cosmic origins. It is this world, the spirit world, that will have to give them their conscious future.

Here we once again see that early childhood, when allowed to develop in the "two-world" consciousness, can be a key to the true purpose of the human being. The circle can express hidden seeds of social awareness. Souls in the spiritual world that are nearing a new earthly life prepare themselves for this new life under the guidance of higher beings. These souls form groups or circles according to their affinities and goals. By committing themselves to similar tasks and purposes as well as through their inter-relational development, these souls can form strong bonds of solidarity. These groups come together again on earth at a certain point or under certain circumstances to live or work together. This can also happen in childhood. For example, certain souls come together as kindergartners to jointly experience the descent to earth out of the spiritual world. In later life, these souls may belong to completely different groups, but in kindergarten we can feel which souls have similar tasks. Led by the kindergarten leader, the soul content that they brought with them will take on earthly form. This will be carried by them throughout their lives on their individual paths.

All experiences of the soul that come forth from tasks, desires, and ideals, and also from "soul debt," and which working together bring the soul to certain deeds or actions, form what is called "karma." Groups of people that find each other through karma are called "karmic circles."

Some people will feel that they have met many of these karmic circles during their lifetime. However, that they exist between kindergarten-age children, and even toddlers, is something new. Previously for young children daily life and therefore karma only took place in the home, but now it has extended to pre-school and kindergarten. We could also say that when souls stand at the threshold of birth and choose (or are assigned) a certain family, they now need to choose a kindergarten leader as well as find kindred souls also looking for this leader. It is understandable, of course, that they do not have to do this all by themselves, but are led by higher beings.

Even though we ourselves cannot yet fully understand these relationships, we will have to agree that the karma of toddlers and kindergartners has expanded and that a completely new realization of old karma and forming of new karma has been made possible in this age group. Group circles that hardly existed a hundred years ago, such as kindergartens with their group leaders, can now be searched for in the pre-birth spiritual world. At the same time, new bonds and relationships must be formed to allow karma to follow its path. What used to take place only in the spiritual world now takes place partly on earth, forming new possibilities for the future. In the middle of this new development stands the young child, who now has a completely new task in the forming of human relationships. This will be discussed further in the final chapter.

Sometimes we can have the feeling that the "soul family," the karmic soul group, is present in the intimate atmosphere created in the kindergarten group. Sometimes this feeling of "family" comes forth more clearly in its circle element through singing a song together (perhaps accompanied by the group leader on the lyre), or while listening to a fairy tale, eating a sandwich during the break, or playing a singing game together. By using the circle element in such a game the hidden bond between these souls can be expressed even more clearly.

It is fascinating to see that every "circle" has its own character. Eating together gives a domestic feeling and an earthly bond, and in this activity human relationships can be observed. The circle of the fairy tale could be seen as a childlike version of "medi-tation" (from *medi*, *medium*—being in the area between heaven and earth). The singing game, connecting heaven and earth, can also have an element of a "hymn," and can represent a singing abandonment to the spiritual world, as mentioned earlier.

However, the circle clearly shows its other side when part of a singing game. Where we first felt the dangers of social awareness at too early an age, we now feel that the circle can also be an intimate and protecting cloak for the young child. This is the reason that of all the singing games, the circle game is the one that can be played with the youngest kindergartners. Because of its intimacy, the little ones can easily be helped and guided where needed, making sure that the less positive influences are turned into positive possibilities.

To better understand this, we should think of what we discussed earlier regarding the transition from "dream rhythm" to "deed rhythm." This is seen to a large extent in "back-and-forth" games (see Chapters Six and Seven) and the still-much-too-advanced "line" games. Let's look at "I would make a string of beads." In this singing game, the children walk hand in hand or with arms linked, symbolizing the slowly awakening possibility of linking thoughts. By means of physically linking the arms and legs, the brain is partly freed from this process, giving the (soft) rhythm the chance to steer these thought processes in the right direction. But the little ones who can hardly stay in the line can feel lost and helpless; where is the intimate circle?[6] We should therefore not ask the newcomers and the youngest children to join this game. For them the best game is a quiet circle game that still envelops them and, if they don't want to play, allows them to sit quietly sucking their thumbs. They must be given time to watch and join in when they are ready, so that they are not rudely awakened from their precious early-childhood dream.

Of course, the reader should understand that there are no clear boundaries in the differences between the games nor in the division that we have made here. For example, "White swans and black swans," with its beautiful spiritual character and floating rhythm, is played as a line game, while the already quite earthly and rhythmical "Have you ever heard of the seven, the seven. . ." has much spiritual content and is played as a circle game. What is important is that we find an adaptable norm in movement that despite its flexibility is the common theme through the world of games. Thus we are asked to use the games with sensitivity, according to each child's development.

6 | Form, movement, sound, and repetition

Everything that has been discussed until now shows us that singing games are made up of many different elements. For example: image, movement, rhythm, form, melody, the sound of words, and so on. We will now look at the elements of form and movement—circle, two groups moving back and forth, line—from a different point of view, whereby we will be able to create a threefold grouping.

We have seen that when properly used, the circle element of the singing games, but also of the kindergarten as a whole, has an enveloping, supporting, and protecting character, on a human as well as a superhuman level. If we open ourselves to the enveloping character of the circle, we may finally reach the deepest origins of all, the power that carries each soul, consciously or subconsciously: God the Father. It is this all-encompassing power of the Father, which still envelops young children, that comes to them in earthly form as soon as they feel ready to join the circle. Contrary to the rhythmical waves and constant movement of other games, and even though children may still walk around, we feel that the circle gives room for the element of fatherly peace. This is the ancient element of Peace, the living, shaping Peace of the Father from which all else comes forth.

Rhythm is the primary element of the "back-and-forth" games. It is the principle of life that is revealed in our pulse and our breathing, but also in all great earthly events: day and night, summer and winter, high tide and low tide. It is that which leads humanity and the earth in its development, the pulse of life on earth, the foundations for the Son. Even human souls need the rhythm of closeness and separation to create a bond. These first signs of the life and development of the Son are what cause deeper human understanding and love to be born and grow. The principle of going back and forth in the game portrays the way relationships between human beings grow rhythmically.

The next type of game, creating figures while walking in a line, forming a long "chain" or "string" (as in "i would make a string of beads"), can be seen as an image for something much larger. Doesn't it illustrate the essence of logical thinking? To what even-deeper origins can this take us?

When humanity lost access to the illuminating and revealing character of the Spirit, the only way in which the spirit could still express itself in life on earth was through one-sided earthly logical thinking, a straight-line-logic kind of thinking. Growing children learn to connect their earliest cosmic experiences in this earthly way, much as the links of a chain or a "chain of thought." The line represents the beginnings of the spirit, albeit in rudimentary linear form. It is not until much later in life that the essence of the spirit will be freed and revealed again.

It is our belief that of these three types, the singing games in the circle are the first that are suitable for smaller children. There are even some group leaders who think this type of singing game is the only one suitable for kindergarten-age children. However, since groups are made up of various ages and all the singing games have a place in these years of development, it is up to the leader to decide which games are played when and by whom. If all the games are used, the last two types will have to be adapted more than the circle games, and should only be chosen for the older kindergartners. All singing games have their place; in one class they may be implemented faster than in another, and each leader will have to follow his or her own instincts to know which one fits the group at any particular moment.

After the difficulty of the strong rhythm in the "back-and-forth" games, as discussed previously, having to conform to a line is the biggest problem in the line games. This conformity is emphasized by the fact that the leader must walk at the front of the line and therefore cannot help the little ones if needed. The feeling of being enveloped that is present in the circle games, and partly possible in the back-and-forth games, is completely lost in the line games where it is actually needed the most. Letting the youngest children participate in the line games will almost certainly harm them. Therefore, if played in kindergarten at all, this type of game should be reserved as one of the final ones to introduce.

Everything is easier with the older children, but don't forget that *all* singing games were created by school children. Keep in mind that while the slumbering powers of intelligence and rhythm should not be awakened in the youngest ones too early, the older kindergartners should not be asked to use these slowly-awakening powers too soon.

Remember that young children first lived at home playing with dolls or blocks. And then they were brought to a kindergarten, where they first experienced and were asked to function in a group. This unnatural way of being brought together and being "kept busy" was made even worse by implementing singing games meant for school children. Here lies an important task for every kindergarten leader: to rethink and rewrite the games to fit the group. This re-creation certainly already takes place in many kindergartens (see Chapter Ten), but we sincerely hope that more games will be developed that fit these young children. Such games would envelop the rhythmical element in more warmth and less with active deeds, so that the "chain of thoughts" is illustrated more effectively.

If we ask ourselves what young children understand of the words of the singing games, we will quickly come to the conclusion that they are not much more than "word sounds" to them. This does not mean, however, that we understand more of the intention of the words than the small child. Imagine an opera in a language that you know nothing about. When I heard an opera in Russian, a language that I do not understand, the music and the completely new way of singing and acting as well as the sounds of this Slavic language fascinated me. Not understanding the language made me more open to the other elements. It seemed as if something of the entire Slavic people wanted to be revealed. We will all have had similar experiences. Don't we encounter a wonderful tableau of sounds in nature every day, whose words we cannot understand but which reveal completely new elements? The clouds that pass in the sky, the wind in the trees, the rain that splashes on earth—don't they all reveal cosmic mysteries to us?

Young children have a similar experience when seeing and hearing singing games of which they understand little or nothing. Their experience is much larger and more real than ours because they came from a world where the language of the spirit was heard. It is the "spirit recollection" that they hear in the half-understandable "word sounds" of the game.

Sometimes many years later, when the child begins to understand the words, a strange disenchantment might take place. Through that which was "mis"-understood as a child, through the lack of simple logic, something of the super-logical mystery of the "other world" came through. And this was much more understandable and much greater than the logical meaning. A kindergarten leader once told me that she attended a religious school as a small child and that she learned a greeting that was said to the prioress. With complete devotion she said: "Father and Mother Prioress, greetings!" The respect that she felt in saying these words was so great that she never questioned the logic of what she said. The world of the Father, from which she came and which still surrounded her, but which was not represented in the form of a man in the boarding school, was still honored in her greeting. With her words she filled the gap of that which was present in her spiritual but not in her earthly life. It was not until much later that she understood that the adults did not say "Father and Mother" but "Worthy Mother Prioress," a realization that had quite a sobering effect on her.

This half- or "mis"-understanding when listening to songs, games, or verses lasts much longer and is more important than with fairy tales, in which understanding the words and their meaning is necessary in order to follow the story. This is why fairy tales are not suitable for toddlers. Singing games are also premature for very different reasons, as discussed earlier. Word sounds remain close to their cosmic origins, and the word connections are still so elementary in these games that the child experiences them as sound phenomena which sometimes take on a magical character. The magical experience of the game continues for a long time through the connection of the word sounds with melody, movement, and rhythm. Finally, when basic understanding is slowly mixed with this magical experience, the spiritual element in a child can be so great that the logical does not overrule the illogical. It is not until much later, towards adulthood, that a conscious view of all of this is formed.

I once heard from a young man who can still remember the precise moment shortly after his early childhood when he discovered that word sounds in the games had a specific meaning, for example that the sounds "s-t-a-r-s" meant the stars in heaven. Soon after this realization, he tried to correct his younger sister, then in kindergarten, who sang the words of a song differently than they should be. She protested vehemently, saying that the words she sang were right. She would not let him take away her "sound magic."

The older singing games allow kindergarten-age children to live the word sounds much more intensely than do the newer games. This should not surprise us if we think of the role sounds have in the old games. We feel that these old games originated while playing, not only with arms and legs, but also with sounds instead of with a logical combination of words. The content hidden in these sounds often has an imaginative character, much like what we find in fairy tales. Thus these games will not feel strange to the children in the kindergarten, and will certainly only do them good. Other elements belonging to the age of school children, such as deed-rhythm and form, should be kept away from the younger ones.

If we want to create new singing games for these children, we should not forget the importance of the still-so-strongly-present word/sound experience. And in order to give them the "word music" that they need, we should go back to the old singing games that can teach us this element that is so healthy for the kindergartners and that used to belong to the schoolchild as well. At the same time, "creating" a new singing game, in other words "allowing it to grow within us," happens together with the children. Games born out of this inner playing will not only be focused on what is best for *these* children but will also be the most fruitful in word sounds, melody, and movement and therefore also in content. As mentioned before, the melody should be based on the pentatonic scale (G-A-B-D-E) rather than the more common diatonic scale.

It is possible to create a game especially for one child who needs some extra attention or care, as long as it will also work positively for the other children. In this way games can be created in each group that have a very specific character but also have a more general meaning. The (positive) influence that a game has on the children, like all of their experiences, will not be seen immediately. Usually the impressions are buried deep in the soul only to surface much later, sometimes not until adulthood. They then show what positive or negative influence they have had on the life of a person. Who knows how many impressions are internalized but never become conscious?

Something else that works unseen is the silent attention that we give to children when they are not present. Our preparations for the following day, when we are thinking of what we will do with them or what we will ask of them, have a direct influence upon them, because our soul connects with their souls and gives attention to their specific needs. When done regularly, the result can be a peaceful foundation for the inner development of the children. Re-creating old games or creating new ones works in the same way, as long as we always keep the children in our heart. Again, these experiences grow unseen, creating invisible relationships between the children and us.

Each of us alone may not believe that the quality of what we make will have any effect at all on today's world, especially when compared to what was produced by early humanity, who still lived in direct contact with the spiritual world. This should not divert us from working on the task at hand with joy and devotion. The most important thing is that we work towards our goal. Higher powers will help us take the first steps in what we need to do for the children. How will our descendants feel if they see that one or more generations before them had become resigned to inactivity? This question can help us to keep on searching for possibilities in the spiritual realm, and also in the world of fairy tales and games. We will discuss this point further when we look at some newer games in Chapter Seven.

It is important that we keep the old singing games alive. However, this will not be an easy task, especially since these games need to be adapted to make them age-appropriate. But once this is done, it will help us come closer to understanding what the games contribute to the development and, more importantly, the essence of the young child.

The old singing games, in their wholesome folkloric character, can be seen as little folk mystery plays, much as the mystery dramas by Rudolf Steiner are for adults. These dramas show us how to rediscover the way from the earthly to the spiritual world via thinking and schooling. In much the same way, cheerfully and freely, the old singing games show children the right path to take from their origins in the spiritual world to the "workplace of the soul," earthly life. (See also Chapter Nine.)

When looking at the magic of word sounds, we wanted to emphasize that the old games have certain formative elements that we seldom see in other games, and that keep us at the brink of or above the "abyss" of earthly logic. Humanity had to fall into this abyss to develop earthly logic, but must now try to rise out of it while maintaining and deepening the acquired inner consciousness.

In order to form a clear impression of the imaginative language of the old folk games, which is almost an expressive painting with words, we could look at the fresh absurdity of a line such as "Fair Anna sat on majesty, majesty, majesty. . ." (see Chapter Seven). What should we do with such a song in our modern, business-like lives? The first thing we notice is that the song is protected from rational understanding through its strange choice of words. Since rational understanding would prohibit us from understanding the real content, the strange words should be appreciated. Children enter into a "thought fog" that can be very meaningful. Some collectors of these old games go so far as to see an irrational choice of words as the hallmark of authenticity and will only then add a game to their collection. The absence of outward logic, which we may appreciate by itself, can only reach completeness when juxtaposed with the presence of more hidden content and other qualities in a game. If this hidden content reveals itself in and around the riddle-like words, it will not lead to disappointment when the child's consciousness awakens and the meaning of the words is revealed. His original experience will either be confirmed, or will be enhanced by an even broader content.

It should be obvious that we should never correct the words a child uses in a game or song. We should never forget that kindergarten-age children should be allowed to continue living in their dreaming world of sounds and words and that they are not yet ready to "learn" in the sense of structured school learning. The profound meaning of the old games works subconsciously in the deep hidden soul of the child and slowly, sometimes much later, awakens from its wanderings to an enriched understanding.

But what is the deeper, hidden meaning of these games? Let's take the singing game "I must wander." Although it may be logical to put something that is dramatized in the present tense, there are many children's games that are in the past tense. The present tense gives a game an inner as well as outer sense of "now," while the past tense can give the feeling of being outside everyday reality, in a fantasy world, or even a supernatural world. In fairy tales ("Once upon a time. . .") the past tense has exactly this role. Children who play and are in their fantasy world will always use the past tense: "You were the mother and I was the father and you were the baby and we lived in this house. . ." Sometimes once the preparations are done (and with that often the game), there is a place for the present tense, but this immediately takes a step closer to outward reality: "Could you give me the bread?" or "Don't come home too late. . ." In singing games the tense can be chosen much more freely since the mood is largely created by the musical elements as well as by certain words. In the above-mentioned singing game, although the key is major, the melancholic melody and the word "wander" give the children the melancholic sense of "being lost" that they know from fairy tales.

Here are the words of the game (for the music, see page 142):[7]

> *I must wander, must wander,*
> *Over hill and under.*
> *Here comes a merry little jumping jack,*
> *He's (she's) waving with his (her) hat,*
> *He's (she's) stamping with his (her) foot!*
> *Come let us jump and dance, and dance, jump and dance,*
> *But the others they must stay and stand.*

In this game the children stand in a circle together with their leader. One child, wearing a high hat, walks (preferably with another child or with the teacher's helper) around the outside of the circle while singing the first line "I must wander, must wander, over hill and under," alone or together with the other children.[8]

Until only a short while ago, the first line of the song was reality for the child. His soul "wandered" in the spiritual world, looking at the earthly world from above and wondering where he could find an entrance to the earthly world, in other words, where he should be born in the "earthly circle."[9] While "wandering" in the spiritual world the "hills and valleys" were the hills and valleys of his soul, and they will become the hills and valleys (happiness and trials) of the life that lies before him.

The slightly melancholic melody expresses the homesickness for the spiritual world, the Fatherland, and being sheltered by the Father. It is what we see as the twilight of the gods in Norse mythology; having to leave "home" in fairy tales like "Hansel and Gretel," always followed (very importantly) by being lost in the woods. The human soul, after having left the Father, first gets lost in the spirit darkness of earthly life.

During the game, the circling child enters the circle through an arch made by two children while singing in now cheerful, strong major: "Here comes a merry little jumping jack!" The newborn has passed the birth passageway and can start his life on earth; he is a little colt in what is for him a new earthly environment. Now the group helper can rejoin the circle or dance with the child, depending on the character and age of the child.

Next we hear: "Waving with his (or her) hat. . ." as the high hat is raised and waved as a goodbye to the spiritual world and a welcome to the new life. With "stamping with his (or her) feet," the child makes contact with the earth and is fully incarnated.

The child now chooses another child from the circle, aside from the leader or the helper who are only helping hands, and dances around while singing: "Come let us jump and dance, and dance. . ."

Humanity wants to learn to move freely on earth, but "I" has become "we": moving freely together, not alone. Human beings want someone else to accompany them, but this does not have to be a life partner. More likely it is a karmic encounter of two or more people, but more importantly it is the other person to be with the individual human being, not as "I" but as "we," searching to make a life on earth together. "But the others they must stay and stand": the souls that are not yet ready to be incarnated must stay in the spiritual world until their time has come.

The meeting of two worlds that toddlers experience in dream consciousness plays an important role for kindergarten-age children too. They experience it to a lesser degree, and also in a different way, but it is nevertheless important. If we stay with the singing game we just discussed, we can imagine that after having re-experienced the movements of the soul before birth, singing the lines "I must wander, must wander, over hill and under" gradually shows them the years to come. In everything that they hear about life, "wandering" can become an image for finding their way on earth.

At the end of the singing game as we described it above, the high hat is passed on to the next child and so the game can be repeated ad infinitum. This repetition is seen in almost all singing games. But why is repetition so natural and important for children?

When we think of the enormous cosmic content the soul brings from its pre-birth existence, content that should be given a place in earthly life, we will understand what it means for children to be reminded of this through the old singing games. They will not only remember, but will also look for a way to incarnate it in their earthly life.

Something similar happens in the world of fairy tales. Fairy tales bring their cosmic content not in rhythmic melodies or movement but in a contemplative way. Thus the two complement each other. We also see that healthy kindergarten-age children cannot get enough of either stories or singing games. They *know* that the deeper contents of their souls can find a new earthly haven through both. For this reason the element of repetition is so important.

However, repetition is different with fairy tales than with singing games. In the games, this can be demonstrated by the natural rhythmic foundation, almost like our physical heartbeat or breathing. Much as physical rhythms are essential, so is repetition of the game, for the game itself as well as for the child. It is therefore understandable that the old singing games have this element of repetition in their nature. If the instructions for the game do not include repetition, it will seem completely natural to add this element, so that each child can have a turn.

Fairy tales do not have this type of repetition. Here we only see the repetition of a few words or a verse; there is no ending that allows for repetition. Only the entire fairy tale can be retold, and then retold a number of days consecutively.

And yet we should be careful—the younger children should not be woken from their "dream rhythm" and forced into the "deed rhythm." This will only have negative consequences, as discussed before. Some children also need less repetition than others. Once again, we will have to observe the group closely to make sure to stop before the older children get bored and destroy that which has been created.

The question of whether a variety of games can be played in turn should now no longer need answering. We should not interfere when soul content tries to be disclosed in certain words or movements. If the images created are suddenly replaced by others, the atmosphere that was created will be disturbed. This is also true if the new images are similar to the previous ones. Milk from two full jugs cannot fit into one jug of the same size. The milk will spill onto the floor—it will not find a vessel to fill and will be lost. Similarly, you cannot ask a child to be able to divide one soul content into two different images. Every spiritual image needs to be given full attention and obviously cannot be sent in two directions. Play one game ten times, but do not play two games five times each. If you do, you will encourage superficiality by jumping from one to the other without ever deepening the experience, and the magical processes of the game will become degraded to simple amusement. Depending on the group, some games can be repeated for days on end, thus allowing the soul content to identify with the game images. But keep in mind the nature of the various children so that you do not overdo a good thing. A gentle balance is needed when playing these games—too much creates chaos in the soul world of the child. And here we see another parallel with fairy tales. Too many different tales will result in the same type of chaos, for the very same reasons.

Another parallel can be found in the preference that some children show for a certain fairy tale or game. This can be so great that a child continually asks for that tale or game. We call this preference the "favorite fairy tale" or "favorite game," and it represents an interesting phenomenon in a child. After all, every fairy tale and every game brings each child's particular motives of the soul and expresses them in images as well as in movement and melody. However, each soul has its own special development that is thus expressed in the "favorites" of the child.

In general these preferences are for games and fairy tales in which the soul finds a connection with its hidden content, nature and task. The child's favorite game or fairy tale contains that which the child already carries within, since the workings of the game or tale will only be effective if such a connection or relationship exists. If possible, it would be good to give in to these personal wishes if the group allows it. How to give in to the preference of one child without denying another is a question of tact, which can only be obtained through years of practice. One should always be careful that the preference is healthy and not an obsession. Here we will have to rely on the children themselves, that the healthy constitution of their souls will help them find the right balance in order to create a suitable "haven" for their "soul content."

If we look at the larger picture, we could say that many souls, probably those that have the most important roles to fill in their future lives, are deeply convinced of the inner tasks that they have received and have brought with them from the spiritual world. What they seek intuitively, especially as young children, and what interests them the most, are the actions, words and images that remind them of these tasks. Once this is understood, the preferences of certain children can be met with confidence, as long as we let ourselves be led by the karma of each child.

It is interesting to consider the story of Saint Martin at this point. Saint Martin, the great benefactor and propagator of Christianity, was the son of pagan Roman parents. When he was a boy he had a Christian governess who told him endless stories of Christ and the child Jesus, not because she wanted to but because he repeatedly asked her for these stories. We may recognize something of the workings of karma as discussed earlier. Through karma these two souls looked for and found each other—one, that of the child, with the task of bringing his inner Christ forces and love to mankind, the other, that of the governess, to create a doorway to earthly life for this unique soul, thus giving it the possibility to realize the task it was given.

As we know, in our modern lives, some parents are not able to continually take care of their children (like Martin's parents) and so entrust them to someone else. If this caretaker, be it a governess or kindergarten leader, decides to help the possibilities slumbering in the children to find their way into the child's earthly life, then he or she will certainly feel an affinity to Saint Martin's Christian governess. In this example we see both types of karma: that of the past, and that which leads us to the future. As adults, especially those working with children, we should understand the importance of both these movements.

Aside from repeating the singing games physically, there is also a slightly different, although no less important, element of repetition in the games. The repetition of certain lines or refrains has something very special that repeating the whole doesn't have, and that is *variation*. Something can be created step by step by repeating the words of a line or refrain differently each time, whether in movement or intonation. In Chapter Seven we will look at two songs that show this more clearly.

Step-by-step creation through repetition is the fountain of life, of the world, and of the development of mankind. Each new development phase repeats the previous phase and builds upon it. We can see that the deeper soul life of the child not only carries the cosmic sources of his own rhythm of development but also the rhythmic development of the entire world. The pulse of becoming human and of life on earth beat together with the rhythmical phenomena of the world as a whole. Therefore how can we possibly distance ourselves from this element of rhythmical repetition, and shouldn't we be thankful that the games bring this element of repetition to our children?

7 | Types and examples of singing games

Even as we go further into the background of singing games in this chapter, we should keep in mind that our focus is on the *experience* of the kindergarten-age child. While working on this book, I came across a quotation that is attributed to Dr. Ita Wegman. These words inspired me to continue my work on the subject that we are currently considering: the importance of understanding the young child and the future of humanity. What we believe Dr. Wegman said is written on the opening pages of this book: *Man müsste einen Kreuzzug machen nach dem Wesen des Kleinkindes* (A crusade is needed to find the essence of the young child).

These words are given even deeper meaning if we compare them to the story of King Gilgamesh of Babylon and what he experienced during his search for eternal life. After endless roaming he comes to a far-away island (read: the spiritual world) where he finds his forefather Utnapishtim. Utnapishtim gives him an herb called "Old Man Grown Young" (cosmic life still present in a young child can be won back by the adult who consciously works on inner development). However, this herb is stolen from him on his way back home (to the earthly world). Now, since "eternal life"—the bond with the spirit that has remained present in young children until today—was completely lost to adults after the time of Gilgamesh, we are urged by the quotation above to rediscover the essence of the young child. This will undoubtedly be the salvation not only of the soul of the young child, but also of the "eternal life" of humanity.

While looking at the singing games in this chapter, we should try to keep all this in mind and attempt to put ourselves in the shoes of a kindergarten-age child. We would like to win back the "Old Man Grown Young" miracle herb that Gilgamesh lost, insofar as that is possible in modern times.

We will not discuss too many games at this point, as that would distract us from our focus: the essence of the young child. A few from each category will suffice to teach us to understand the imagery of the games themselves. If the games that are discussed inspire further personal development, we can only be thankful.

We will begin by looking at some old games from the inner experience of the kindergarten-age child—the unspoiled, still partly cosmic child. We start with the game type most suitable for this age group, in which the "Father-element" is strongest: the circle game. It is interesting to note that this is the most common type of old singing game, suggesting that the people who originally played this type of game still lived in a collective consciousness.

Circle games

Lay my hankie down (for music see page 143)

A beautiful game, partly akin to "I must wander," which we discussed in a previous chapter, is "Lay my hankie down." The words are as follows:

> *Lay my hankie down*
> *Don't make a sound*
> *I was watching the whole night through,*
> *Made myself two pairs of shoes.*
> *One of cloth and one of hide,*
> *Here my hankie shall abide.*[10]

The children and their leader sing together while standing in a circle holding hands. One child (accompanied by someone if necessary) walks around the outside of the circle holding a handkerchief. It is not important that this child sings; it may even be better if she doesn't! The children in the circle close their eyes and, while they are closed, the walking child places the handkerchief behind one of the other children and walks away quietly. The children then open their eyes and the child behind whom the handkerchief was placed tries to catch the first child before she reaches the now-open spot in the circle. If she doesn't make it she gets to go again; if she does, the second child who chased her now has a turn.

Although there are similarities with "I must wander," the content of this game is quite different. In the game discussed earlier, the "wanderings" show the circling of the soul before birth in melody as well as in movement. In this game, the wanderings are shown less in the melody and more through movement. This also clearly illustrates finding the right place in which to come to earth: "Here I lay down my handkerchief!"

But what about the handkerchief? It's a pretty mundane item. What does it tell us? It is indeed mundane for us, but not for the young child—on the contrary! A handkerchief is very light, and in spite of its lightness absorbs our breath, an image that the kindergarten-age child understands. Breath has always been connected to the soul as well as the spirit. God gave Adam the breath of life, that of the soul and the spirit. In Dutch there are two expressions when someone passes away: "he exhaled his last breath" and "he gave the spirit." (In English, "He breathed his last," and "He gave up the ghost.") In Greek "pneuma" means breath as well as spirit. Thus we see that this so-called mundane object can mean so much more for a child, as it reminds him of the soul and spirit element, and through this element he looks for a healthy entrance to the earthly world.

From the very beginning of the game the child only thinks about finding a way to let his soul content come to earth: "Lay my hankie down." There is no talk of hills and valleys here. The emphasis is on the intimacy and the mystery in which these things must take place: "Make not a sound."

The next lines show the intense spirit work that the "I" must perform in the pre-birth spiritual world to prepare for the coming earthly life: "I was watching the whole night through, made myself two pairs of shoes. . ." The incarnating soul must have the right shoes for life on earth. The farmer must put on the right boots to work the land; in the *Kalevala*, the hero Lemminkäinen must bind cloth around his legs to protect himself from vipers while plowing the field. In the same way, every human soul that comes to earth must be well prepared for harsh and sometimes painful or harmful relationships: the soul needs good footwear to be able to fulfill its task during its life on earth.

However, in this game the soul has made *two* pairs of shoes: one of cloth and one of hide, or leather—in other words one for the lighter, and one for the more difficult path ahead. This reminds us of the hills and valleys of the previous game. Our shoes must carry us not only through pleasant times but also through times when we are put to the test—through dark as well as light karma. While under the care of the hierarchies our soul uses that which is available to prepare itself for both paths: cloth and leather.

Now that the searching soul has found the country, community, and family in which it can harbor its cleansed soul or breath element, its first task has been completed.

The following part in the game, "playing catch," is less interesting. Of course it is good to have fun during a game, but it should not have to be sought in such an inappropriate way. This part seems to have been added to introduce the element of repetition. It is always important to introduce this element, but a more natural and significant way could perhaps be found.

When compared to the previous game, we find it strange that the child who has just had a the turn *must* play again if caught, while the child chasing her must play if he is too late. In "I must wander," the next child is *chosen* and has the possibility to have a turn. In the one game the child *may* but in the other *must*, which seems imperfect and impure.

There is one last point in both games that should be discussed. In "I must wander," we focused on what the group *as a whole* experienced. We tried to understand how the children wandered around the earthly world before birth, finally descending to earthly humanity. We saw how the children experienced this dreaming adventure while singing and playing in the circle. If in "Lay my hankie down" we look more closely now at the child who has a turn, the lead character—an element that is not kindergarten-like at all—we may be able to feel something completely different. When the child leaves the comfort of the circle she may experience a sensation that is anything but a return to the nurturing spiritual world. More likely she will feel lost and alone, a feeling that can only partly be taken away by the helper accompanying her. We once again see a side of the singing games that shows us that they are actually for older children. Much thoughtfulness and care is needed to play these games, even though they are the ones that come first for the kindergarten-age children.

Luckily, the relationship between the child who walks around the outside of the circle and the circle itself is quickly restored. The attention is on the circle, albeit from the outside. The child now asks herself how she can step back into this community. As long as this question is answered cheerfully and peacefully, she will once again feel comforted, not only by the children in the circle but also by the spiritual world that has accompanied her through her lonely wanderings. She has not been left on her own.

This leads to another point. Children of kindergarten age, who should still be allowed to be somewhat "antisocial" (that is, should be allowed to retreat into their own world), will also experience what the group as a whole goes through while playing the games. This is an experience that can be seen as a dreaming preparation for the community spirit that is developed in later life.

For us adults there is also something special to be experienced here. By deepening our intimate understanding of young children, we can rediscover something of the miracle herb lost by king Gilgamesh: "Old Man Grown Young." The world that the children bring with them, full of cosmic soul content, is (seemingly) lost. However, some of this content can be rediscovered through the years. This used to happen fairly automatically as one grew older. Today this richness can be rediscovered much earlier. Aside from the increasingly materialistic mindset of humanity, there is an intense will to rediscover the inner self, and also to rediscover the essence of the child. This development is happening *before* growing old, even in the first stages of adulthood, and gives us the chance to rediscover something of our own early youth. In the same way, the kindergarten leader will not have to wait for gray hairs before being able to find something of the lost miracle herb of Gilgamesh, as long as she opens herself to her group wholeheartedly.

The seven leap (for music see page 144)

We have chosen a completely different but no less interesting game to discuss next. "Have you ever heard of the seven leap" is played as follows: The children walk hand in hand in a circle and sing:

> *Have you ever heard of the seven, the seven,*
> *Have you ever heard of the seven leap?*
> *They say I'm not a dancing man,*
> *I can dance like any nobleman!*

At this point the children stand still, let go of each other's hands, face the center and, while making a gesture chosen by the leader, sing:

That is one...

Then the children walk on, repeating the first verse, stand still and now make two gestures, the first one followed by an added new one:

That is one. That is two...

In the end there are seven gestures to be done, always the old ones followed by a new one, preferably gestures that bow down further and further until the child is a small ball, which represents becoming one with the earth, becoming a clump of earth. At the very end everyone jumps up and the game begins again.

Let's first look at the numbers. Today, we see numbers indifferently, one just following another without any specific value. This has not always been the case. Previously, human beings understood the character of each number. The Egyptians saw the number one as the largest of all. For them, oneness was total unity, which when divided became a multiple. They set *one*, an indivisible number, against *two* and gave *one* a "male" character and *two* a "female" character. The Egyptians and other ancient cultures saw each number as an independent being. Without going into all the numbers we will jump directly to the number *seven*. When we speak of a certain development, large or small, this number is important wherever the element of *time* is important. According to spiritual science, the entire development of our earthly world, which is represented in the biblical Book of Genesis as happening in seven days, takes its course in seven great planetary phases, each of which consists of seven parts, and these parts again encompass seven epochs each. Spiritually, human life is built up of seven-year periods. And finally, humanity in general shows a sevenfold development.[11]

Since the game we are discussing also shows a certain development, it is no wonder that the number seven plays such an important role. Here the sevenfold development is seen as a *leap*, or jump, presented as a *dance*, a "nobleman's dance," not an everyday dance. We could say: a *magical dance*, using the word "magical" in its original, positive sense.

Actually, there is only one truly positive magical art of dance, an art of movement that works creatively and directly out of pre-existence in the spirit into space, and which can only be made visible by someone initiated in these mysteries. This is the art of eurythmy. Eurythmy enables the creative spiritual word to reveal itself in human physical movement. It is not a human creation, any more than speech is. Even though translated by humanity on earth, both audible and visible speech (eurythmy) stem from a divine principle, which we could call the Spirit of God. Thus we can learn to understand how alongside the words from Genesis ("And God said, 'Let there be light,' and there was light") and St. John's Gospel ("In the beginning was the Word"), Rudolf Steiner could say that creation stems from *World Eurythmy*. With what we know about the essence of eurythmy, we can understand that this statement includes what is presented in both passages from the Bible, but characterizes creation as more of a deed.

This "world creating" artistic movement, originated and still being realized by God, and meant to be led further by mankind into a World Eurythmy, can be perceived everywhere around us if we have the ability to do so.

In the game of the "Seven leap," every verse goes deeper into physical movement, contracting further and further toward the earth until the children are little balls, which are then freed by jumping and stretching up. Without going into too much detail, we could say that we see a similar contraction and expansion in the evolution of the world. At present we are obviously in a phase of deep descent out of the spirit, a "contraction" out of which we hope to once more be freed into a higher and freer plane of spiritual awareness. Fairy tales often show a return to the spiritual world after having been lost. Little Red Riding Hood and her grandmother are swallowed whole by the wolf but are later freed from the wolf's stomach. Hansel and Gretel are lost in the woods and put in an iron cage by the wicked witch, but finally helped by a white swan, which returns them to the "world of the Father." Snow White is freed from her wicked stepmother's grasp by the kiss of a prince.

In the "Seven leap" game, physical movement accentuates the element of rhythm, and contraction and extension are experienced seven times, each time more intensely. Once again, this must be brought to the younger children with care and subtlety in order to avoid exaggeration—but the older children in the kindergarten will experience it with great joy. Here the children can physically experience a darker aspect, as well as the element of repetition, in a way that is not possible through listening to a fairy tale.

Let's look back at the larger context of time in this game, the "planetary development" as given by spiritual science. In contrast to the other two games we have discussed, and aside from what the human soul personally experiences in its growth, we see that the development of humanity as a whole is important for the child. The larger world evolution is still present in all of us; for adults this may be merely a theory, but for children it can come to life subconsciously through a dreaming experience of certain singing games.

Where in fairy tales "seven-ness" is brought through images and imagination, in games it is brought through rhythm and movement, which also engage the will system of the child. This will make a more intensive schooling and stimulated development of the soul possible in later life. Regularly seeing and taking part in the sevenfold world dance as a young child will help the adult find an entrance to the "seven leap" of soul and world development.

A pretty little mirror I have found (for music see page 145)

A beautiful and profound circle game is "A pretty little mirror I have found." The children once again stand in a circle, while one child (see note 8) walks around the inside of the circle with something around his neck that represents a mirror (do not use a real mirror, as this will limit the child's fantasy). Everyone sings the following song together—please substitute pronouns and names appropriate for the child who is playing:

> *A pretty little mirror I have found*
> *Upon my heart I'll have it bound.*
> *About-turn, about-turn,*
> *And who does this about-turn?*

During the last line, the child chooses another child from the circle and hangs the "mirror" around his or her neck. The chosen child now turns around (looks out of the circle) and the children sing:

> *Our John has turned himself all about*
> *From another child he found it out.*

(That is, from the girl or boy who gave the "mirror"). The two children have changed places and the second child (Jane or John) now goes to the center of the circle, while the other children walk around hand in hand and sing:

About-turn, about-turn
And John does his about-turn.

When the children have stood still and turned inward, the game starts again and the child who was given the "mirror" walks around the inside.

Originally the fourth line of the song was "Pretty Jane, turn around" and only used girls' names. Modern kindergarten leaders will agree that boys' names should also be used! But let's look at the motif of the "pretty girl" in fairy tales. Here we see that the male element is the active *spirit*, usually represented by a prince or king, while the female character is seen as the receptive *soul*, the princess or "lovely girl." Thus it will not surprise us that this game, which clearly wants to show us the development of the soul, uses the image of a "pretty girl."

Using something or someone as a "mirror" or example can be seen as a soul task, and this is demonstrated in the game. Every soul that comes to earth has the task of acquiring self-knowledge. This is often done through "mirroring" ourselves. We should not only come to know our positive and negative qualities but also learn to look for and recognize tasks and impulses that have been hidden to us for ages or even eons. It is the flow of karma in our life that constitutes our hidden personal path of development. When studying ourselves, or another person, this is where we should address our questions. Probably the most comprehensive way in which we can come to self-knowledge is to fathom the profundity of "humanity," of which every human being is a part. We should look for the Christ-indwelling "We," in the sense of the personal comprehension of our consciousness, as opposed to the twofold (larger and smaller) personal "I." Every human being has the task of looking for this largest form of human awareness.

For the time being it will only be possible for us to achieve self-awareness by finding ourselves and others mirrored in everything we do and experience on earth. By mirroring ourselves in everything we do, have done or want to do—and in everything that we experience, have experienced, might experience, and in everything that happens in the world, has happened in the world and may happen in the world—we let the essence of our own self and humankind grow. We must be completely convinced when we sing "A pretty little mirror I have found." We must be able to say truthfully to ourselves and to each other: "Everywhere around me I find and have found little mirrors that reveal the mysteries of my deeper self and of the human self to me." We must *bind* these revelations *to our hearts*. The words "Upon my heart I'll have it bound" must also become truth. Then the larger "about-turn" from appearance to reality can manifest itself in us when we look at ourselves and the world as a whole. Only then will we be able to learn to see the deeper meaning of ourselves as well as the whole world. Nietzsche called this "the re-evaluation of all things" (*die Umwertung aller Dinge*).

John the Baptist warned, "Repent, for the kingdom of heaven is at hand" (Matthew 3:2). He did not wish the people to change from a belief in multiple gods to faith in Christ, as one might think, but to turn to the deepest primal knowledge of all things. This was not just a new belief, but the deepest possible "change of soul content" and *about-turn of the soul* from earthly appearances to inner spiritual truth, through which one can meet Christ. In the deepest sense this is what "about-turn" means after the "mirror" of self- and world-knowledge—the mirror of the soul—is received by the soul, held up, and looked into.

Every child who comes into the circle and binds the mirror to his heart will turn around. In a larger context, every human soul that truly mirrors itself will accomplish its own world-encompassing *about-turn*.

There is another side to this "about-turn" that we should consider. We could think that the kindergarten child who is still so much connected to the "cosmic land of the Father" in his dream consciousness repeatedly turns to his soul past. Isn't this what is meant by *turn all about* in the song? But we should understand that the "about-turn" in the game is the act of self-mirroring and that this must be *learned* ("from another child he found it out"). This is something the child can only become ready for in the future as an adult; it is not a memory of the cosmic past. Remember that the child who turns around first faces the inside of the circle and is surrounded by his group leader and the other children. On turning, he faces "nothing" outside the circle, certainly not a return to the security of the Father-realm. Although less intensely than in "Lay my hankie down," the child will most likely feel a loss of the security just experienced when facing the inside of the circle.

With his words "Repent, for the kingdom of heaven is at hand," John the Baptist longed for a renunciation of simply merging with higher powers. He hoped that each human being would look for and realize the Christ impulse on earth. But in order to rediscover this impulse, human beings must go through close examination of the "I." This goes hand in hand with working through deep valleys. The game shows this in a childlike way that might be too much for some of the children to handle, especially the youngest of them. If there is no helper in the group, it is important that one of the older children accompany the younger when he turns to face "nothingness," walks around to choose the next child, and hands over the mirror. Once again, here is an example of how each game must be made to fit the group.

Regarding the mirror, we could ask ourselves: Aren't we all, when we open our minds, larger and smaller mirrors for each other? We can see ourselves mirrored in all other people and they in us. A young child cannot be aware of this. However, the actions of giving the mirror away and on the other hand receiving it, giving another child the possibility to turn around, will have a certain meaning for both children that they will experience in silence. We should be thankful if we were given the chance to sing and play these games in our youth.

Flowers blue in meadows green (for music see page 146)

There are two more circle games we would like to discuss. Aside from the element of human relationships that many of the games share, this one also shows a fresh element of nature, which has its own character. The words are as follows:

Flowers blue in meadows green,
Lovely as the silver's sheen
Flowers in garlands wound,
One dame (or gent) must skip and bound.
One dame (or gent) must still and silent stand,
Then three times round is our command.
And the dame (gent) s/he must kneel before a friend
To start the game all over again.
That will be, that will be, that will be our (child's name).

The children sing while walking hand in hand in a circle and one child stands in the middle, once again accompanied by an older child if necessary. After the third line, the children stand still and the child in the center dances with "a skip and a bound" (it is best to have decided on the exact movements to be made beforehand to avoid crazy movements caused by shyness). After the dance this child stands still and then walks around the inside of the circle three times and chooses another child in front of whom he or she kneels while the children sing "That will be our (insert child's name)." The game now begins again with the chosen child in the middle.

This simple game refreshes us with its blue flowers resembling silver and woven into a garland. It brings us back to real life and the actions of mankind. Here we can play, dance, stand still, and go around three times in a world of plants and minerals. Finally the soul kneels before someone else and makes room for someone new.

Together with the child we experience the transition from the pure physical-etheric world to astral human actions, represented by the dancing in the game. However, this "skip and bound" when performed without a full "I" consciousness resembles that of a little goat or calf in the "meadow": it is not yet fully human. Consciously coming to a standstill as well as to conscious movement can only be achieved by the human "I" ("three times round is our command"). And only a human being can show respect for another human being by kneeling, thus giving the new person the leading role, something we all would rather keep for ourselves. Seen in a larger context, the personal, small "I" can make place for the larger "I" of humanity that lives in the other as well as in ourselves. It is this that can enable us to search for our highest "I," the Christ "I." In this simple game, the first subtle steps in this development are seen in the act of choosing another child and giving him or her the lead. The game shows us the line of evolution from earthly plants and minerals, via the astral component shared by the animals, to human consciousness and human morality, and finally to the highest possible in us, the Christ principle: "not I, but Christ in me." As in the "Seven leap" game we see the rhythmically-danced sevenfold development of humanity, this time mirrored in the various aspects of nature and in the lower and higher levels of humanity, eventually rising to the Christ in human beings.

In summary: the "I must wander" game gives us pre-birth soul strength with which to find our (personal) way over and under our lives' hills and valleys; the "Seven leap" lets us rise above the hills and valleys and join in the creation of the world, as will the divine, creative human being of the future;

and "Flowers blue in meadows green" brings us the entire development of the world and humanity, from its earliest origins to the present as a "world drama," and from the present to the future as a Christian-moral path of development. It gives us a clear view of the past and loving, moral guidance for the future—the road from the beginning to the end.

Fair Anna (for music see page 147)

The last circle game to be discussed is one that brings us to a central point in our development. This is the peculiar game "Fair Anna." This game impresses us not only with its length but also with its unusual choice of words.

The children stand in a circle with "Fair Anna" standing in the middle. They sing:

Fair Anna sat on Majesty, Majesty, Majesty,
Fair Anna sat on Majesty, Majesty.

(Only the first words of the following lines will be given, as one can easily complete them by following the above example.) While "Fair Anna" stands in the center, now with her hands before her eyes as if she is crying, another child, representing her mother, leaves the circle and walks to her while the children continue to sing:

And then her dear old Mother came...

The "mother" now sings alone (or with a helper or the leader):

Say, Anna, why are you weeping so?...

Anna says (also accompanied if needed)

I weep because I have to die...

Mother: *Why do you have to go and die?...*

The children now sing further while "Frederick" steps forward:

That wicked Frederick, he did that!...

He has just gone and made her dead...

Now she's been put into a box...

But look, she stands up happily...

Now she becomes an angel pure...

The angel chooses another child...

The first few of the above lines should not be acted out too realistically, as we will discuss later. Once "Fair Anna" has become an angel and has chosen a new child, the game begins again. Of course, a boy can also play Anna. The name may be changed if desired, but as the content is about the human soul, the words "fair Anna" can be kept for a boy as long as he doesn't mind.

It will once again be interesting to note that the strange first lines have no effect on the children (as discussed in Chapter Six). The word "majesty," for them still unknown, is experienced as a sound and does not pose any problems. Here we see another example of the "sound magic" in which young children have their own dream-experience that goes much further than any logical explanation could. Such a dream-experience allows them to make a connection with the deeper meaning of the game.

It is through experiencing the sounds that children can best come to an understanding of the words. For example, in this game they feel that the strange word "majesty" illustrates the soon-to-come "return to life" of Fair Anna. This does not need explanation, and may later be connected to the actual definition of the word. This type of presentation of words is closely related to the larger encounter children have with language from the moment of birth, which leads to a deep bond with the living spirituality of language.

When looking at this essentially very serious game we would like to return to the mirror game (which was not included in the summary above). In the mirror game, we experienced how the soul can work on itself, thus becoming a co-creator of the world. The game "Fair Anna" teaches us how the slumbering forces in us, the Christ forces, that allowed us to *turn our soul around* in the mirror game, can now help us *rise out of* the inner loss of spirit, out of the inner dying that modern life threatens ("that wicked Frederick"). It teaches us that we can rise up out of this soul death and come to a life that is devoted to the soul, new for us and for the world. Thus the future soul of mankind ("Fair Anna") can accomplish its task, together with the nine higher hierarchies to form the tenth spiritual hierarchy. It will then become "an angel pure."

An unusual relationship between form and content can be discovered through what is revealed to us in these games. We have been looking at circle games, which we have previously said belong to the Father type. However, the content is full of moments of resurrection and thus can be seen as belonging to the world of the Son. This is something that we have already encountered in the mirror game, although there it was less pronounced. The twofoldness in both games shows us that differences between the form and content of the games should not be taken too literally. Combinations and variations can enliven and deepen the meaning.

An important detail that we should not forget is that the "death" caused by "wicked Frederick" should not become too realistic. Anna should not be killed, something that should be obvious as we are dealing with children in the kindergarten. This is not only because such actions may awaken harsh and sadistic feelings, but more importantly because the game then loses touch with what it is actually portraying. In this context "dying" is sinking into soul darkness. Little Red Riding Hood is merely swallowed whole by the wolf; she is not taken by his teeth and torn to shreds. She just disappears. This is the language of the imagination. In "Fair Anna" we could represent dying by having Frederick cover Anna with a black piece of fabric. This is a representation of inner death—being locked out of the origins of the soul—and will be understood subconsciously by the children. The line "Now she's been put into a box" could be substituted with something like "Now she's been covered with a shroud."

The resurrection of the soul, or its rising up to new life as an "angel pure," much as Little Red Riding Hood and her mother reappear out of the stomach of the wolf, poses no real problems. Anna can simply pull off the cloth. However, there is one element of this game that should be looked at closely by every group leader individually: the element of "evil." Evil is needed before good can be achieved. Without the wolf, Little Red Riding Hood and her grandmother would not have been able to descend into the depths but would also not have been able to rise up again. Likewise, "wicked Frederick" is needed to allow Anna to rise up to the light of the spirit. Without Pontius Pilate, who sentenced Jesus, and the executioners who nailed him to the cross, He could not have risen in that particular way. But who wants to play the part of "evil" and stand in its place? We would rather not give a definitive answer to this question. When playing this game each leader must look at her own group, following her own ideas and instincts, and should feel free to adapt it to the needs of the group.

In relation to this question, we should look at the dark element with which the name Frederick becomes identified. This is especially strange when we look at the origins of this name: "Fried-rich," literally translated "peace rich"—a beautiful name. Be careful with the name, as it may become a symbol of darkness within the group. One of the children might be called Frederick, or a brother or good friend. Therefore it might be wise to change it to something like "big, bad man" or anything else that fits.

All in all, this game can be seen as a "circle game of resurrection." We should not dismiss the drama as unfit for the kindergarten, but use it tactfully so that its cosmic content can find its way into the lives of the children and become the foundation for later subconscious ascension. However, children who are still closer to toddlers in their development should probably not be allowed to participate in this game.

Now we look at the next type of game: the "back-and-forth" game, or the "singing and answering" game, in some ways introduced in the last circle game "Fair Anna." The game is now no longer between one child and the rest, but between two rows of children who sing to each other, back and forth.

Back-and-forth games

In back-and-forth games the "Fatherly" cloak that was still present in the circle games is no longer present. It is therefore understandable that this game type suits the older children in the kindergarten better than the younger ones. How could these younger children possibly join in a game that asks for rhythmic movement, when "deed rhythm" only causes restlessness in them? We have already seen that dreamily *watching* such games, or periodically looking up from their own play, can be good for them—as long as they are allowed to remain in their own world.

In the language of game images we see a descent from the cosmic world to the earthly world. Between people we see a rhythm between contact and withdrawal, speaking and listening, question and answer, giving and receiving. This rhythmical back-and-forth in relationships between people is translated into a game for children, with approaching and retreating, or stamping while singing first one line and then another—almost giving the game a ritual character. Doesn't this approaching and retreating movement of human souls come from the world from which all healthy human relationships stem? This world, which we used to call the world of the Son, appeals to our consciousness by way of the game, and it can be experienced even more deeply by the children through the game.

We will only discuss a few of these games, as they are meant for the older children in the kindergarten.

We come from far-off lands (for music see page 148)

The first is a much-loved game about "far-off lands." The children stand in two rows facing each other with a yard or two between them. One row, while singing the first two lines, takes a few steps forward and then back again; this is repeated for the second two lines. Next the other row does the same for the second verse, asking a question. Thus the two lines come towards each other and retreat one at a time; this pattern is repeated for verses three through six. The seventh and last verse is sung by the first row while standing still, and a child is pointed out (selected by the leader). Then the game is repeated.

The text of the song is as follows:

> *We come from far-off lands,*
> *Margo, Margo, Margogely*
> *We come from far off lands,*
> *Margogely.*
>
> *What have you brought for us?*
> *Margo. . . (repeat refrain with each verse)*
>
> *A basket of golden roses. . .*
>
> *For whom will those then be? . . .*
>
> *They're for my dearest one. . .*
>
> *And who's your dearest one? . . .*
>
> *That will be, that will be, that will be our (insert child's name). . .*

Like many of the games, this one can be played in various ways. We could select a child in one of the rows who will choose his "dearest" from the other row at the end. The chosen child joins the other row and the game starts again, this time with the roles reversed.

Another way to play is that only one child—obviously an older child!—sings the odd numbered verses (using the "I" pronoun) while the rest of the group is in a row opposite him. At the end he chooses one child to join him and the game is repeated, each time allowing the newest child to choose another child, until all the children are in the newly formed row.

The chosen child may also decide upon a new gift instead of the basket of gold roses, so that the precious gift is varied. This is a nice idea, but not ideal for the slightly younger children. They will not be able to think of something new right away, thus disturbing the rhythm of the song. Plus, these children still live almost completely in the imitation phase. Thinking of something new asks for too much abstract thought as well as conscious initiative. In other words, this independence is a premature appeal to the lower "I" and could "awaken" the children too early. It is therefore best to stay with the basket of gold roses. The repetition of this lovely image will not bore healthy children in the kindergarten and will only intensify their experience.

Typical of the change from the circle to this new game type is the change from duple time signatures (2/4 and 4/4) to the more cyclically oriented 6/8 time. This difference in rhythm has various unusual aspects. We know that children who slowly become conscious of *active* rhythm first have access to duple time.[12] This is embedded in the 4:1 proportion of heartbeat to breathing (4 beats to one breath) and in the games to walking on two legs. This twofold rhythm of the legs, when learning or just having learned how to walk, is leading. However, the steps should not become too heavy or earthly, something to always keep in mind.

The threefold beat shows a completely different character. Through its cyclical orientation it represents dancing more than walking, giving it a light and happy feel. But be careful, as it can also lead to lightheartedness to the point that some children will lose themselves. Even if this does not happen, we should be aware of the possibility.

It is interesting to note that the threefold rhythm, especially 6/8 time, which children will not actively use by themselves until much later, is the rhythm used in nursery songs sung to infants. It is as though our ancestors understood that the soul of the young child lingered in the cosmos and must be surrounded by the cyclical rhythm of the stars in the heavens. When looking at toddlers and the youngest kindergarten children, we could say that because they are still very much carried by the cyclical or cosmic rhythm, they are not able to show this element while singing and walking. How can a child show what carries him? Who can lie in a bed and carry it at the same time?

Because the cyclical 6/8 time of the back-and-forth games is only revealed in the song text and not in the steps, many of the difficulties are lost. The older children will be able to step to the beat, but thankfully, the younger ones will continue to have difficulties with it. They will hobble along and let themselves be carried, much as when they were infants. In the past, the cradle was rocked, giving a twofold back-and-forth experience but also a flowing cyclical rhythm. This does not happen anymore; the cradle stands solidly on the ground, but the songs have not lost the cyclical character.

It is fascinating to see that the games we teach our children first are the circle games with their straightforward twofold walking pace, followed by the straight-line, straightforward back-and-forth-but-cyclical games in 6/8 time. For the kindergarten-age children this sequence is fine, because it is about what they carry within and what they can actually reveal. These can sometimes be opposites. This is not only the case with children—it is quite impossible to teach adults who still have a dreaming consciousness to dance a waltz. It is only when they learn to think "straightforwardly," or in an "earthly" way, that they will be able to learn to waltz with their legs.

In a larger context we could say that the world rhythm or proportions that surrounded and filled our souls before birth, and that continue to live in the small child, still flow through our heart, limbs, and entire development. We seldom ask ourselves where these immense things come from. Sometimes we gradually suspect or even feel something of the cosmic origins of these world proportions that still live in the child's soul and continue in us. Then we feel something like the Fatherly foundation of the world and the helping, creating heartbeat of the Son.

Out of our own consciousness we can continue into the larger dream world of the child. We may feel something of the Father in the circle created by the children, and the heartbeat of the Son in the rhythm of the back-and-forth games. We may experience how the Christ-inspired rhythmic element that flows back and forth between human souls can cause us to search for each other and bring humanity together. We will now also be able to understand why it is the "back-and-forth" games, instead of the circle games, that start with the word "we."

If we begin the above game with the "I" pronoun, it will not contradict what we discussed above. The still-to-be-developed "We"-consciousness can only come forth from "I"-consciousness. This is a very large inner step, actually much too advanced for a kindergarten-age child. The image in the game points towards the distant future, much as the "dream of the future" gives the children a foundation for their later-to-be-fulfilled development.

With regard to the content of the game, we need to listen to what the children and the game have to tell us. How true that the children come "from far-off lands"! Haven't they come down from the (for us) far-off cosmos? The people who have fully descended to earth, represented by the second row, can now ask "What have you brought for us?"—a question that every dreaming child poses to another child, and that can be brought to reality through the song. "What riches have you brought with you?" The child can truthfully answer "a basket of golden roses": I have brought great treasures of the soul. The other group asks the next question to which he actually already knows the answer: "For whom will those then be?" answered by: "They're for my dearest one." Who is the dearest for these children of the kindergarten? They can't know this consciously, but we can: their gifts are meant for all of humanity. Everything that the soul has, coming from the cosmic world, is a gift for "humanity on earth," for the human beings that destiny wants the children to meet and who represent humanity in general. The "dearest one" is "the other" who must be willing to open his heart to this heavenly gift. This game is a game that gives and takes in human and cosmic relationships, and can be experienced in the realm of the Son while being supported by the foundations of the Father.

We're the poor Marionsen (for music see page 149)

The second back-and-forth game is "We're the poor Marionsen." Once again there are two rows across from each other, and one row steps towards the other twice per verse. The text is as follows (with a repeating refrain):

We're the poor and needy, needy, Marionsen, Marionetten,
We're the poor and needy, needy, Mari, Marions.

We're the rich and wealthy, wealthy, Marionsen, Marionetten...

I would like to wed your daughter...

I don't have one you can marry...

I had heard that you do have one...

She is not for you to marry...

I shall give her pretty clothing...

It's not enough for you to marry...

Then I'll kneel right down before her (or Then I will give her heaven)...

Well then you can go and wed her...[13]

Much as in the previous song, the text changes from the "we" form to the "I" form, resulting in a back-and-forth between the two groups with repetition. In the text, we may also be able to sense a childish prelude to Fatherly origins, human independence and maybe even something of Christian love of humanity. Understandably, when looking at the text, this game can only be played if both rows sing their lines and cannot be played with only one child across from the group as in the previous game.[14] The seventh verse ("I shall give her pretty clothing") can be varied at will with different gifts, only to be refused by the other group.

Finally the offer of "heaven" is sung while one of the "rich" boys kneels before one of the "poor" girls and is accepted. The girl then joins the boy in the other line. As in "We come from far-off lands," be careful that the things offered fit the song and game. Once again the child who offers something should not be "put on the spot," and the rhythm of the song should not be disrupted.

It is interesting to note that in this game the soul descending from the spiritual world is seen as poor, while the soul on earth is rich. This is quite contrary to the text of the previous song, in which the new soul brought golden roses. Here, the new ("poor") soul must beg for the earthly ("rich") bride and is even refused! In this difference, something of child development during the kindergarten years can be seen. In the "far-off lands" game the souls were not asked to bring or offer anything from their "far-off" higher origins. The second row, representing earthly humanity, only asked *what they had brought*. In the "Marionsen" game, a roaming young man, played by the entire row, asks for the hand of the beloved "daughter" almost immediately and offers all kinds of gifts in order to win her. Here, only those watching can ask themselves what kind of riches he is hiding in his "basket of roses."

While younger children will experience this game in a dreaming state with all its cosmic dimensions, the older children in the kindergarten are already full of expectations and desires for the coming life. They are actively playing, no longer dreamily, but actually "putting things into practice." In other words, the older children bring their cosmic "gifts" in an active way through play to the earthly world *themselves,* making this world increasingly their own. Thus these two games express a transition in the development of the young child.

In the "Marionsen" game one could be inclined to see an inwardly impoverished earthly human being who wants to rediscover something of the lost, rich spiritual Fatherland. After all, this is something that happens on earth. But this occurs between adults, not between children. Only adults, who feel that the pre-birth, Fatherly soul origins to which they had dreaming access in early youth are now closed to them, can consciously endeavor to rediscover this spiritual world. If translated in this way, the children's game becomes a game for adults.

Adults who become conscious of their inner poverty are in the sense of Christ "poor of soul," but, through being conscious, open themselves to the possibility of an inner, spiritual rebirth. Young children can never be "poor of soul" in this sense. They still carry the riches of the Fatherland within them, and have the subconscious task of giving these riches to the *earthly* world. And, as previously mentioned, they long for this new world so that they can take the next step in their development. They long for *our* world, which will bring them their future. Thus for young children the "rich bride" is the earthly world, a world in which they in the *earthly sense* are still "poor," but to which they want to give their gifts, and even bring "heaven" if needed.

But what about the girls? How can they look for a "bride"? The most obvious answer is that girls as well as boys can enjoy this game. We can appreciate that children, insofar as they understand the words, know that the game is about all of them "coming from heaven" and searching for earthly life. Verse 9, however, which may be played by two children, would then most naturally be played by a boy kneeling in front of a girl.[15]

Much can be explained when we look more closely at how the meeting between the poor soul and the rich father develops. Through all the refusals we can understand that the cosmic gifts the descending soul has brought with him for his "bride" (for life on earth) are not actually enough. We need to aspire to and achieve more earthly things. Interestingly, the final acceptance then turns upward, to "heaven." In addition, the act of kneeling down brings us back towards the soul but also lets us take a step towards adulthood, something we should be aware of when playing this game with children in the kindergarten. What does this motif do for them?

Even for adults, kneeling down has various connotations. We feel that our daily "lower" consciousness, while indispensible on the one hand, can be a hindrance if we want to open ourselves to something greater. We may have to come down from our "I"-ness, become humble, and spiritually "kneel down" in order to be open-minded. Spiritual kneeling can also become a physical action, although we must always ask ourselves if this action is pure. For kindergarten-age children, though, there is no question of becoming humble on the inside or of kneeling spiritually. To expect this of them would be forced and fake. For the children, kneeling is purely part of the game, especially across from another child. Only when it is done in play will the children be able to take something of this experience with them into later life.

Of course, kneeling for earthly things, for earthly beings, and bringing offerings in order to achieve something one wants can have another character. One can kneel for the material, earthly world, and forget or even betray the soul. In our adult world this can also be seen as "kneeling before the rich bride," an aspect that we should not overlook. The children in the kindergarten do not know this world of mammon, nor do they live in the anger of the wolf in fairy tales. Nevertheless, the wolf comes and swallows Little Red Riding Hood and her grandmother whole....

In the fairy tale, the dark woods and the big, bad wolf represent the deeply hidden anger that is present even in the souls of little children, which receives release after enduring and passing through the images of the story. In the game, there is no big, bad anything, and everything is sung and played joyfully. The deeply dramatic light and darkness, or rather "light–dark–light" of the fairy tale is missing here. Thus we can surmise that the dark mammon-being that is deeply hidden in every human soul is not addressed in the joyful play of the game. Through such cheerful play, the children can't have anything but a healthy longing for the earthly world, for the "rich bride" awaiting them.[16]

Even for adults the game can be a positive guide, but in a different way than for the children. With every new environment, children subconsciously recognize something of the soul content they have brought with them. We adults can only rediscover this with great difficulty and probably only through conscious will and spiritual schooling or practice. Through conscious schooling we can understand the images created by the game and endeavor to open ourselves to our surroundings. While kneeling is only play for the children in the kindergarten, for us it can become an image of conscious devotion and surrender to the cosmic content of all things on earth. We can try to rediscover what the child subconsciously experiences, but is now so difficult for us to open ourselves to.

We must learn to listen to that which wants to speak to us silently. We must try to find what we can contribute toward human development. Only then can we become part of something that will become reality in the far future: the reincarnation, in the earthly world, of the slumbering soul. By bringing this "wedding gift" to earth, by consciously giving thought to her silent soul words, we adults will be able to make her our *true* bride. Playing the "Marionsen" game in a purely childlike way in kindergarten will contribute to creating a sound foundation for this endeavor. Thus we see that this game, with all its different facets—its manner of searching for and reliving the soul in the earthly world, its human relationships and rhythm, understood subconsciously by the child but consciously by the adult—must be experienced in the light of the Son.

Line games

Following the cosmic elements of the circle games and the rhythmical, human relationship-building elements of the back-and-forth games, we are ready to look at the line games. This type of game lets us stride along with everything that moves in time. The path of human life and the movements of the day, large or small, can be found in these games. There is something else that gradually starts to awaken in the older children in the kindergarten: logical thinking. In these games child logic is shown through the movement of the legs, one step after another.

At the same time, we may be reminded of another type of thought in which something of the general human soul could live in ancient times, but which has withdrawn from our modern reasoning: the hidden ways of the cosmic Spirit principle in the world. Such cosmic world thinking was once the foundation of all the dreams of humanity, and it still weaves itself through the dream-thinking of children. It also lives in what children *do,* and *walks* with them if the line games are played with a dreaming consciousness.

The Spirit, as with the Father and the Son, seems a large name to use for such games for young children. However, we will have to understand that the subconscious connection of the child with the Spirit is large enough to justify the use of this name. We should therefore not be afraid to use it, and should see the line games as being in the light and in the continued work of the Spirit.

I would make a string of beads (for music see page 150)

The first line game we will discuss is "I would make a string of beads." In this game, walking in a line happens in a somewhat unusual way, causing the tail of the line to get stuck right away. This happens because the last child (once again this must be one of the older children) puts his free hand high onto a wall, thus creating an arch. The leader as "head" of the line walks through the arch taking all the children hand-in-hand with her. The more children she "pulls" through the arch, the smaller the arc of the line of children gets, so that eventually even the other arm of the last child has gone through. The arc is gone and the last child has gotten himself in a knot! His arms are now crossed. Now the second- and third-to-last children make an arch with their arms and the next child gets himself into a knot, and so on. In the end the whole line is "knotted," a "chain" is created and, if the line is long enough, the leader can take the hand of the child who stood against the wall and create a circle—a "string of beads." If the children now let go of each other's hands, we are once again in the circle and the game can start again with a different child at the tail end. The song that is sung while playing this game is:

I would make a string of beads,
But I lack the thread I need.
Ha, ha, victoria,
Ha, ha, victoria!

Because this meaningful game uses the "I" form it should most certainly only be played by the older children in the kindergarten. In its structure and content we see unusual contrasts. The difficult and lengthy nature of the movements is in sharp contrast to the short song that will have to be repeated often during the game (see Chapter Six for the value of repetition). Making a chain or "string of beads" reminds us strongly of a logical chain of thought and therefore touches the children in their sensory perception. That the "thread" was not available will seem quite acceptable to us but will not be experienced consciously by the children. Nor will the cries of "Victoria" mean anything to them, but because they are preceded by "Ha, ha" and accompanied by a joyful tune, the children will understand the triumph that is expressed. A strange game, full of contrasts!

Let's look at the melody—something completely different. The back and forth of the first notes (despite the fourth interval) is almost a dreaming, rocking rhythm that the younger children will certainly recognize. The joyfully accentuated ending is much more harmonious than we would expect from the sudden jump in the text. These milder qualities in the melody soften the sharp contrast in the words and the movements of the game.

Obviously the game must end on a positive note, as we expect from fairy tales, thus making it understandable that the text does not end with the fact that the thread is unavailable. However, as the solution does not come from the content and can therefore be seen as slightly untrue, we should be careful that the joy expressed in the last two lines is contained so as not to become cheeky "behind the scenes." If contained, the joy expressed at the end can become more thankful for what has "come from above." The fourths used in the melody, with their earthly character, can give a positive note by bringing the dreaming, rocking rhythm of the first two lines more to earth. If done tactfully, the transition will thus be softened and become a valuable addition to the game as a whole.

There is one significant problem with this game. That is the fact that the leader must lead the line of children and can therefore not help the younger ones who will almost certainly have problems with a number of aspects, not the least of which being that they have to tie themselves in a knot![17] This asks for a helper. But at the same time, the children who are too young to participate must either be kept busy or be accompanied while looking on (think of the streets of Rotterdam). They also need a helper. Thus, if we want to play this game in kindergarten, we really need two helpers unless all the children are of an age that they can all participate, which is rarely the case.

So what are the positive aspects of this difficult game? Why, with all these reservations, can it still be important to the development of the child—for the older ones directly, through active participation, and for the younger ones indirectly, through observation?

We know that everything that focuses on earth has a strong attraction for the child who is searching for earthly life, and this includes the earthly chain of thought. But what will the child experience? The ability to consciously connect thoughts has cosmic origins; although the children in kindergarten cannot do this yet, there is a certain connection with their pre-birth origins. It is a type of "magic," much like that we described earlier with regard to sounds. But in what direction does this "magic," this hidden but also exposed work of the spirit, go?

In our daily lives we can see how the hidden thought element made its way to earth through the many different weaving, knotting and threading techniques. These knots and fabrics were never consciously invented. They show us an earthly intelligence that came from the spiritual world, a "magic" that can only be observed from the outside and cannot be fully understood. This spirit principle that has been interwoven or threaded into our earthly life is what this line game wants to express. First we had "sound magic," now we have "knotting magic."

As a child, when I came to a new school that gave attention to the arts as well as academic subjects, I was suddenly surrounded by children who knotted and strung all kinds of things together, making useful objects such as belts, bracelets, and bags. It was as if I had entered another world, and in my childish dreaming consciousness, it was a miracle how a one-dimensional thing—a string—could be guided in such a way that it acquired substance and turned into something so beautiful. I felt that the knots could not have been invented by humanity, nor could they have come into being by themselves. In my childish way I felt certain that they must have come from some supernatural intelligence. Through the knots I encountered something of the binding element of the spiritual and earthly worlds, long before I was able to understand this consciously.

In myths and legends the knot or twist also represents how spiritual intelligence became earthly logic. Think of the Labyrinth of Crete, or the Gordian knot that Alexander the Great could not disentangle and eventually cut. Alexander was not ready for cerebral thinking and therefore acted out of his will.

Since the knot has become an earthly object for humanity, it works in both positive and negative ways. In the positive sense, we work with this unfathomable world magic daily, whether in the home, the textile industry, or fishing. In the world of the soul, we can "tie the knot" and connect ourselves with another human being. In the negative sense, we come across the knot in everything that is out of our league, whether on a physical or soul level. A belt, rope, or ribbon can get tied in a knot. If a relationship between us and another human being, or even our own inner soul life, becomes too intricate it becomes a knot.

In a larger context a "knot" can also mean asking for and at the same time pointing to a new future. Isn't all of humanity in a spiritual "knot" right now, and aren't we all looking to untangle this knot?

In the past hundred years we have found a new meaning for the essence of a knot, a meaning almost opposite to the meaning of the Labyrinth and the Gordian knot. The disentangling intellect, which for Alexander lay in the future, is now everywhere. Perfecting it further would only send us back into the maze.

There is something else that we must try to achieve. Isn't it true that new karma can be formed from deeply entangled knots of the soul? Of course many such knots will have to be undone, or cut. But there are others whose "task" is not to be untangled or cut but to be brought to a higher level. In earlier times relationships between people were characterized by the rule "an eye for an eye, a tooth for a tooth." Now, if someone has undergone a major injustice, he can forgive instead of taking revenge. This change in attitude makes way for new possibilities in the relationship between two people. If we have done something wrong, we can now forgive ourselves instead of tormenting ourselves, thus bringing ourselves to a deeper level. In this way the "soul knots" are elevated to a more intense and higher karmic connection, a Christianizing karma. Like the knots that children made at my school, which were not made to be undone but to create a new form, our soul knots can be dealt with in such a way that they create new Christian karmic connections. Our future must be made up not only of untangled knots, but also of a refined fabric of soul knots.

This is why the leader makes a new circle from the "knotted" children, thus creating a "necklace" before repeating the chain game. Since the children make the necklace together it can have an even greater effect on them. Couldn't it be that many of these souls have already been together for quite some time and have further to go together? In every line game these parallel karmas can find each other. In the circle game this common karma was also visible, although in a more static form. In line games there is a united movement towards a new future.

It is interesting to see that in this game the group of souls makes (soul) knots together and looks for a solution by bringing the soul knots to a higher level: a new circle, a karmic circle of knots. Thus the Christian-social-karmic development is seen in children's play. This new development is what the older children in the kindergarten feel subconsciously. The younger ones experience it as a phenomenon of the world and humanity through their open eyes and souls.

Line games alone do not allow children in the kindergarten to experience togetherness, or community spirit. This is probably the reason why the line games that they like best are the ones that also have the element of the circle, or are *mixed*. This is what we see in the chain game. The following are two more examples that show new connections in the "way of humanity."

Between France and Germany (for music see page 151)

The first song is about a *goal*, and the *road* the group will follow that will bring them to this goal. Contrary to the previous game, reflection and more intimate understanding arise and create a longing for the circle, which is then finally formed. It is striking to see that the joining group element is so strong in this game. It is often played while standing still in a circle even though the song is about the road, the goal, and even "moving towards" this goal.

The words are as follows:

> Between France and Germany
> Lies the road to Rome.
> If you wish that way to fare
> You must learn our manners there.
> You must learn our manners,
> You must learn our manners,
> If you wish that way to fare, you must learn our manners.

End:

> All who wish that way to fare
> Now may stand in Rome so rare.
> Now we stand in Rome,
> Now we stand in Rome,
> Now we stand in Rome so rare,
> Now we stand in Rome.[18]

The song is about that what is known and already experienced in life, the relatively close-by countries (in relation to Holland) of France and Germany, and the unknown road to far-off Rome that must be followed *together*—"All who wish that way to fare." But the road can only be followed if things are done in "our manner." The road to the future can only be followed if life is lived and understood in a certain way: the road to Rome, the spiritual ideal of medieval Europe.

Why is it that this game, which asks us to follow the road to self-reflection, still makes us search for the circle element? What does this song do that makes us develop from the "I"-form of the previous song to the binding "we"-form used here? What gives us the feeling of an intimate group?

There is one thing that can give us a hint. In ancient times, people could still feel that souls were brought together for the purpose of working or living together. This predestined road of life to be followed together can give people a strong, unified feeling. It is this bond that is expressed in this song and that gives it the character of an intimate circle.[19]

Even in children, in their dreaming subconscious, we can detect these feelings. Moreover it is interesting to note that what is played so innocently by the children can harbor a certain reality for each of them as well as for the group, including the leader: a hidden reality that can become a life reality through play.

The game is played as follows: the children stand hand-in-hand in a circle and walk around for the first four lines. They then turn towards the center, let go, and show their "manners" (through a movement that was thought out earlier).

While walking in the circle, as in the circle games, keep in mind the 6/8 time of the song. This is also a strange thing. The most-loved circle games are in 2/4 or 4/4 time, and 6/8 time (stepped in two beats per measure) is normally seen in back-and-forth games. In this game, 6/8 time is walked in the circle. This is easy, of course, but in the back-and-forth games it has a dancing character, something that does not fit a game about the road of life. Obviously the dancing character of 6/8 can easily be avoided by stepping calmly. The first four lines could also be stepped in 4/4 time, which gives it a better character, although it should not become trudging, nor marching. It is up to the leader to guide the game in the right direction so that the children walk along life's road together calmly.

Another thing that should be kept in mind is that once a game is played in a certain way, it should not be changed. We can change the *mood* ever so slightly if needed but the *form* should remain the same. For adults it is good to change a habit once in a while. This can create plasticity in our inner life. But for children who are still looking for an entrance into the earthly world, this is not the case. Once part of the soul content has found a certain home it "incarnates" to a degree and should be left alone.

However, a completely different game, or fairy tale, can give another home to the same soul content. This can be very productive as long as it doesn't become too much. Changing the "home" of the soul content can make the children insecure and cause them to "lose their ground." Instead the same form should be repeated frequently, giving the children's souls the best and most peaceful possibility to find their entrance into the earthly world.

Aside from the content of this mixed game, it can also be categorized with line games through its musical element. When compared to "I must wander" or "Lay my hankie down," this game, with its conscious search for the "way to Rome," has a strong line game character and should really only be played by the older children in the kindergarten. If the younger ones do join in they should definitely be observed closely, especially when showing the "manners." While walking around the circle, they should be free to show their own "way" and not be forced to keep to the beat. They should be able to toddle along in their own dreaming manner.

Another way to play the game is for the child to the right of the leader to step forward and make a gesture (obviously this should once again be done together with the leader or helper if the child is uncomfortable in any way). The other children copy this child while singing "You must learn our manners there." The first child then joins the circle again this time to the left of the leader and the game can begin again. Finally, after every child has shown the others his or her "manners," we arrive in Rome: the common goal for the group has been reached. For the final verse, the words of the song can be changed to "All who wish that way to fare, Now may stand in Rome so rare. Now we stand in Rome. . ."

But what about these "manners," these "ways"? What do they tell us? When a group of human souls has a karmic connection and endeavors to go down the mutual life path of their interwoven fates, certain binding life standards are automatically formed. A "manner of getting along," of working together to reach a common goal or ideal, is created. However, this may not be a conscious bond. The group of people that formed around Goethe must have had different goals and habits than the group surrounding Napoleon, for example. Every company, museum, circus, school, or charity where a group of people works together says to the world "These are our ways." Each group forms its own ways or "manners" that also show their common hidden bond.

The distinct hidden relationships in a group of kindergarten children can become evident in the images of a game. Keep in mind that these relationships are much more easily seen in free play than in organized games. It is therefore not the relationships themselves, but the fact that they exist, that is important in the game. The deeper meaning of the game can be understood and remembered once the children reach adulthood, and will contribute to their personal inner development.

When playing this game, it is important to keep in mind that making up movements or "manners" can be difficult for kindergarten-age children.

Children of this age find their way in this new world by consciously and subconsciously mimicking others. They are not yet capable of giving an example. It goes against their nature if this is asked or even demanded of them and will feel wrong because they are not yet ready. A healthy young child will therefore do nothing. An older child, who is more aware of the feeling of embarrassment, will feel forced to do something and will usually act silly. Even if some children do not act silly and calmly show their "manners," this is not good for them. It is a forceful move to wake them from the childhood dream. Only if the adult silently gives an example, subconsciously giving the child the feeling of being supported and helped, can showing the "manners" in this game be brought to an acceptable level. Only then can these images find an entrance into the life of the child.

In their development, adults have the task and possibility to find the soul as a person, an "I." In young children, the soul content brought with them can only flow into them subconsciously; the "I" consciousness is not yet present. Once this consciousness surfaces, even when it has been forced prematurely, the stream of soul content coming from above will be stopped and what has not had the chance to flow into the child will remain in the spiritual world. The instinct to imitate does not only help children to learn, but also protects them from having to act independently, which would consciously cut off the healthy stream of soul content.

The "ways" or "manners" that the leader demonstrates, whether cheerful or serious, should not be insignificant. You can do movements representing *Be careful!. . . What did you say?. . . We are strong. . .* or something more profound such as a movement of slowly forming a ball and finally jumping up again (as in the "Seven leap" game).

Other possibilities include gestures of gratitude or refusal, respect or disdain, friendship, joy or sorrow. The children will imitate these gestures joyfully and they will nestle deep in their souls, surfacing much later in life after having been nurtured within for many years. It will be obvious that these gestures should be thought out beforehand and not at the spur of the moment. They should fit the group of children. Also keep in mind that less is more and repetition is essential.

As long as the aforementioned is kept in mind and the game is led with sensitivity (as in the "string of beads" game), it will work positively for the children. What we do see is that these old games should be revised as they no longer fit our more intellectual youngsters.[20] They cannot be played in their old form anymore and should be updated to fit each group. Only through the conscious leadership of adults, through their understanding of the children and their various ages, can these games be an asset to the children.

White swans and black swans (for music see page 152)

The third line game is "White swans and black swans." This game also has a mixed character: the words belong to a line game, but the content shows a strong Father-character (the circle). The words are as follows:

> *White swans and black swans,*
> *Who will sail with us to England?*
> *England is locked up tight,*
> *The key is broken quite.*
> *Is there no smith in the land*
> *Who can help with his strong hand?*
> *Come forth now, come forth now,*
> *The last one shall come forth now.*
> Or: *The last one is caught now.*

Two of the oldest children, or the leader with one of the eldest, stand across from each other, hold each other's hands and create an arch. The rest of the children (preferably with a helper at the front) form a line and go under the arch as many times as the song allows. The penultimate syllable is held as long as is needed until the last child is under the arch and, when there, the arms of the arch are brought down, "capturing" the last child.

Before describing the rest of the game, let's look at the content so far. Birds have always been seen as a symbol of the human soul, which in contrast to the physical body can rise up to the "heavens," in sleep or finally in death. Ancient Egyptians already spoke about the "soul bird" of humanity, and in fairy tales, a bird represents the human soul or spirit. The swan has its special place. At the end of the fairy tale, when looking for their (Father's) home, Hansel and Gretel are carried across the river by a swan. Their souls, led by the spirit, find the Father. In a fairy tale by Hans Christian Andersen, seven brothers turn into seven swans—they temporarily return to the spiritual world. Also the legendary song sung by swans at death—the "swan song"—indicates the bond with higher worlds that prehistoric human beings gave the swan, as a "soul bird."

The children, whose imagination is strongly related to that of ancient humanity, are returned ("sailed") to their cosmic origins, to "England" (in Dutch, this may also be heard as "engelland" or "angel-land") by the "soul bird." Purified souls linger here, the "white swans," in contrast to the besmirched souls that have lost their purity, "black swans." However, the white swans are doomed to descend to earth at some point, thus turning into black swans, while the black swans, having returned to their origin (heaven) can once again be purified and change back into white swans. In the song, pure and impure souls are placed next to one another, but then, thinking about the white swans that have changed into black swans, the question arises: who wouldn't want to return to England or Angel-land?: "Who will sail with us to England?"

But angel-land is not easily reached, especially not for the blackest of swans: "England is locked up tight" and the key has been broken. The old key to the spiritual world, that is, the methods of initiation of ancient humanity, and the more or less spiritual awareness of medieval man, has been lost. Modern humanity must find a new way to the spiritual world; a new key to the gates of the spiritual world must be made.[21] But where is the blacksmith, where is Ilmarinen from the *Kalevala* who can cast a new spiritual key, the "sampo," since Väinämöinen, the old charm singer (representing ancient humanity still connected to the spiritual world), can no longer help? Only the soul that can make this new key may return through the gates leading to the spiritual world *during life on earth* and become a "white swan" *on earth*.

The game now takes a large step in time. It shows us the future when all souls can return to the gates of the spiritual world during earthly life (the raised arms of the two children). "Come forth now, come forth now": let them pass through the gates of the soul, or undergo an initiation.[22] Finally the last child is caught, and the game can begin again. This last child is caught but also "comes forth" to the front of the line. This was the last one in the long line that reached toward the goal, who now comes forward. Isn't it the same in reality? We often see that those who are "slower," those who are less successful, are further in their inner development and thus are actually ahead.

What does the child experience? Being last in line means being at the end, almost forgotten. All of a sudden she is enclosed and sees that all eyes are on her. She goes to the head of the line, or directly behind the group leader. This child is helped to emerge out of subconscious and physical oblivion and come to the front of the line. For us this takes the form of a game, but for her it is a real-life experience.

During the next round, another child is at the end of the line. Everyone will be able to feel the encouraging influence this played "destiny" can have on each of the children.

Another variation on the last part of the game is that the "captured" child can choose something that has been put somewhere in the room by the leader, for example a number of different colored paper keys on ribbons laid out on the floor. The child can choose one of the keys, hang it around his neck and join the leader at the front of the line. After a number of children have had a turn and have chosen keys, the game can be brought to an end by forming a circle in which the "arch" is included and the final lines are sung while using the keys to open the gates of England. The circle of color formed by the paper keys will give the children both a personal "key color" and a place within a common "forging" where they meet one another. These are "mood colors," "soul keys" that come together in an "arch of key colors." The last line should then be "The smiths can all come forth now!" and the game comes to an end.

When we hear the last line of the game, we may be reminded of Matthew 19:30, in which Christ says: "But many who are first will be last." What do these words say about the locked angel land and the broken key?

When we think about the grounds of spirit that guide and carry us and our current earthly life, we could ask ourselves: "Why did the higher leaders allow us to sink so deeply?" If they had prevented this, even slightly, human beings could still possess something of their higher origins and could thus rediscover them more easily.

An answer to the first part of this question could be that if we were indeed prevented from sinking so deeply, humanity would not arrive at the need to really search for the way of humanity. Human beings, when still in the spiritual world and nursed at the cosmic "breast" of higher beings, carried the dormant task to eventually work on their consciousness and personal development as well as that of the world as a whole. These tasks could only be awakened if individuals were able to *personally* meet the forces that are against them, and learn to understand and eventually defeat them. In turn, this could only be possible if the positively helping and leading hands were withdrawn.

When this happened, it was inevitable that the human soul would plunge into a deep abyss and lose all contact with its cosmic origins. While rediscovering, understanding, and conquering his spiritual enemies, humanity can develop the desired conscious life and work out of the spirit.

I once heard someone say: "A person must first become ill to recover." Although I found this funny, it also hit a deep truth. Humanity had to reach spiritual poverty, or become spiritually "sick," in order to consciously rediscover spiritual health. In other words, human beings had to lose their spiritual Fatherland, in order to recover the world spirit out of the human spirit and to find the inner strength to develop and realize the tasks they have been given.

Not only humanity as a whole, but each one of us can see this as a personal task, giving us an interesting link between humanity and individual human beings. Much as humanity began to lose its cosmic bonds in ancient times (in "early childhood") and continued the process of development almost completely on its own, the cosmic soul life of every human child's earliest years must come to an end. Humanity will have to rediscover the life of the soul from individual conscience. In adulthood, human beings will have to personally find the way that they will, or will not, rediscover the spirit. This is determined by each one's own conscious will.[23] On this road of development, in which the world of the Father is lost and is consciously looked for in the light of the Spirit, the Son gives a helping hand. Christ's forces help us in our independent consciousness and stand by us while we consciously re-conquer a spiritual ground from which our reborn strength can work.

Today, we can see an unusual phenomenon with regard to the essence of the soul, a tendency to see this high principle in its most earthly and businesslike form, as the faculty of *reason*. This word is thought to encompass the full essence of the soul.[24] When we take a more cosmic view of the development of humanity it is clear that this tendency interferes with looking for the larger, deeper essence of the soul. In contrast we will be able to understand how the truly spiritually devout are called "the poor in spirit" by Christ (Matthew 5:3).[25] Despite their so-called soul poverty they are on the road to the full essence of the spirit. Thus it will be evident that those who call themselves "rich," the "scribes" of the soul, are actually at the back of the line. The first will be last. However, the "poor of soul," who often feel left behind but also search for the soul world, actually walk at the front: "The last one shall come forth now."

Through these examples, three very different line games have been discussed and we hope have given insight into the various types that can be found within this kind of game. We also hope to have shed some light on those that can be most problematic for a kindergarten group.

Craft games

Circle, back-and-forth, and line games are the main game types when we look at form and movement. In the previous discussions, we have seen that it is often difficult to place a game in one category, as it is often a mixture of two game types. This is especially the case with games that portray a craft or activity. Such games tend toward the use of the circle, an obvious choice because the game is experienced *together* and at the same time the children form a "circle of spectators." Many children are often involved in the activity or craft shown by the game, making a circle even more self-evident.

The Watchman (for music see page 153)

Let's first look at the youngest children in the kindergarten. It is important that the dreaming mood and experience be kept intact. Showing the exact movements of the activity is less important than communicating its essence and everything that works around it. The following game is especially important for these youngest children because of its cosmic character and can also be meaningful for little ones looking on. The game is "The Watchman":

> *Watchman, in the night watch keeping,*
> *Where do you go so late?*
> *I go past the children sleeping,*
> *As the wind blows through the gate.*
> *And my clapper goes clap, clap, clap,*
> *And my footsteps go tap, tap, tap.*

Watchman, in the night watch keeping,
Where do you go so late?
I go past the children sleeping,
As the wind blows through the gate.[26]

This game places the child in the late hours of the evening, when all souls are in the world of dreams. In other words, the sleeping souls approach the world from which they have come and to which the young child is still so close.

When playing this game the children stand hand-in-hand in a circle. One child, the watchman, walks around the inside of the circle rattling a rattle. The children in the circle sing the first two lines and the watchman answers with the third and fourth lines. He moves to the center of the circle. On the fifth line he rattles three times and on the sixth stamps three times to the music, joined by all the children in the circle, who clap and stamp together with him. When repeating the song, the watchman gives the rattle to a new child during the first two lines. This child now becomes the watchman. It is of course self-evident that the watchman is accompanied by an older child or the group helper if still too young or reluctant to play the part alone.

The song begins in 6/8 time with a floating melody. The middle part is in strong clapping-and-stamping 4/4 time, and the final part floats back to 6/8 time. Once again, the youngest children should be allowed to toddle along, not to the beat but to their own inner rhythm.

What is important for the children in this game is the image created. Through their dreaming consciousness, they experience a hidden reality that protects them while in their dreams: Christ. It is not yet possible to talk about Christ when speaking about kindergarten-age children, as they still completely live in the world of the Father. But in their imaginations they are able to open themselves for the protectiveness and the power of the Son.

Shoe the horse now (for music see page 154)

The following song stays in the realm of the young child and has an obvious activity game character.

Shoe the horse now! Who'll do it and how?
John, the smith, so well can he do,
Upon each hoof he'll put the shoe!

The children stand in a circle and three are chosen to portray the scene: a blacksmith, a horse, and a rider. While singing the blacksmith slaps on the sole of the shoe of the "horse" with his hand while the rider holds the horse. Then the children sing:

Clop, clop, cloppity, clop.

The horse is ready and all sing:

And the horsie goes hop, hop, hop, hop!
Hop hop, hop hop, hop hop, hop.

The threesome is now exchanged for three new children and the game begins again.

As mentioned above, craft or activity games are usually also circle games. However, a rhythmical element is added here, not only in the accompanying movements but also in human relationships (question-and-answer play between the craftsman and those watching). The back-and-forth principle plays an important role, even though the game is not played in two lines. Next to the Father element of the circle, the rudiments of the rhythmic element of the Son are added. Furthermore, through the human intelligence needed to perform a craft, which *originally* was superhuman intelligence, the Spirit is included.

Thus these games should not be seen as a fourth type, but more as an all-encompassing type. These games bring something larger, much as the crafts themselves do: the threefold human being. While happily playing, the children are carried by part of the great foundations of the soul that surround us all.

The *work itself* is also something new. Earlier games show what the soul experienced in the spiritual world, how the soul entered into the earthly world and the human relationships it encountered there, and finally human development on earth. Not one showed *labor or work as such*. This is what the craft games do, and in doing so, they raise the following question: What does seeing and play-acting human work do for the children?

When searching for an answer, we should know that the children in kindergarten already carry the sense of work within them, albeit subconsciously. While in the pre-birth world, the children's souls experienced that labor became necessary because of the Fall. At the same time they saw that it is this human spiritual and physical work given to the earth that can change the Fall into a blessing and give humanity the possibility to truly develop itself and the earth. Through the Fall, both the earth and humanity became isolated from the world spirit, but it is this isolation that has given humanity the chance to develop spiritual freedom on earth. This is also called "healing" humanity and earth from "sickness." How can labor encourage this healing process?

Labor means making something that has become rigid significant again. What has become inflexible in the world can be made flexible through labor. A young shoot from an acorn will become rigid wood, and human beings cannot change that. But a cabinetmaker can create a table, or an altar, from that wood, something that is not possible with the young, green shoot. He gives new life to something that has become rigid. This is the real meaning of honest human labor, even for our inflexible, earthly intellect. It is not our task to bring this "petrified" modern intellect back to its "tender youth," to being carried by the gods. We must help to rediscover the world of the spirit while retaining the developed precision. It is the sublimation of awareness and rigidness, although freely living in the soul, that must be brought to our modern understanding by means of (inner) labor.

Then there is the work to be done on our egotistical, rigid emotions, which should not be softened into sentimentality but should be "healed," given new meaning by including the egotistical reality in a new moral warmth. This can then be directed outwards to other people and the earth in general. For example, it is important that a kindergarten leader not think of the children in her group only as "cute," which is a personal feeling. She should lead them with conscious, understanding love and warmth.

Young children carry the essence of human labor in them, and it is up to us to give them the right "soil" in which they can grow in order to eventually bear fruit. This "soil" can be given to kindergartners through imitation of work activities and through relationship-building or community games.

All work that a child can imitate is of great importance for the incarnation process, the so-called "sprouting." By pretending to be a postal worker, nurse, or mother, by imitating setting the table, washing up, or emptying the garbage, the children can find a connection with the practical side of work on the one hand, and also begin moving from the cosmic origins of labor to its earthly counterpart. Through this great transition something of the cosmic-earthly essence of labor can be brought and carried with them in their souls, to become the foundation for their own actions and for the development of their personal consciousness and ideals.

At school, "work" begins. Labor starts to become duty, and it is up to the teachers to make sure that this duty is done with as much joy and enthusiasm as possible. This is where the artistic element can fulfill an important role. In various lessons we can slowly start speaking about work in an imaginative way with the children. New craft games, of a completely different character, can then be played. After many stages, this foundation will allow these individuals to work on and develop their thinking, and give the possibility for their consciousness to grow and blossom.

We should look more closely at imitation and the feeling it gives. Through imitating others, especially adults, children are given direction in their much-desired earthly life. The intention with which we do everything is of the utmost importance to children: with devotion or indifference, with joy or necessity, with openness or aloofness. The way we work is subconsciously absorbed by the children and becomes the basis for their moral-human nature and actions later in life.

As adults, we must therefore live and work in a most natural and moral manner, whether consciously or not, around children. Toddler or kindergartners will internalize our actions when they observe how we lovingly take care of a very young child, and may very well imitate these actions when playing with dolls. Impressions are made and nestle in the children's subconscious in order to surface in a new and personal way later in life.

Thus the children follow various roads to discover the seeds of labor that will grow into the desire to learn a trade or occupation, to learn to work with joy. The roads they follow are: experiencing the role models that can be seen in daily life, their own play, and the craft or activity games we play with them.

The word "occupation" may remind us of how people used to feel a calling to do certain work. Their decision to choose an occupation came from what they enjoyed doing, what occupied them. Children may experience something of the calling of earlier times through the seeds that germinate while playing. The inner relationship to human labor that existed in earlier times may be revived and may take on a new, more conscious form.

Aside from the inner, partly hidden side of work, we should not forget to experience the practical sides, how working with our hands can create something. Small children have to find their way to the earthly world. How can work without a practical meaning, that does not bring forth objects useful to our earthly life, guide them?[27] A chair, table, or cupboard is built by the cabinetmaker to be useful in our daily lives. It is the earth and not the cosmos that must be "healed" by our endeavors. Thus the cabinetmaker must do his work in a practical and useful manner, in a manner directed at the earth. It is this practicality and usefulness that is seen and heard in the craft games. The question of who will shoe the horse is answered with "John, the smith, so well can he do." In a later game we hear "I am a blacksmith good and true."

Even payment for work can be justified, as long as it is not seen as a "goal" or "reward" in and of itself but as a natural consequence of work done. It is understandable that working purely for payment is not right. Human endeavors are priceless; the work that must lift the earthly world to the next level cannot be a tradable object. We need not worry about this in the games. The good intentions of the group leader and the feeling created by these words will certainly be understood by the children.

For the somewhat older children in the kindergarten the difference between male and female work becomes more and more important. Girls and boys are starting to differentiate themselves at this age and the older girls would sometimes like to act out jobs of a more female character. Traditionally jobs done by men usually had a more extroverted character than jobs for women: they "placed something in the world," while the jobs done by women had a more caring and nurturing nature. This is what we should look for in the games for older girls. An example is the game about *washerwomen* to be discussed later, but unfortunately there are not too many other examples.

In order to give these girls what they are looking for, the leader can make up new games that portray daily life, the life of the farmer's wife or nursing and caring; that is, real women's work. Of course, not every leader will feel up to creating something new. Another possibility is that new verses that sing about womanly tasks are added to existing songs. However, we should be careful when doing this as the younger children may become confused if something new is suddenly added to a song they already know. They will not understand these variations, especially as they *themselves* are still being taken care of. These changes will be seen as disturbing and could do more damage than good. All in all, it is obvious that we must be careful with changes. The best would be if the leader is well prepared and presents the song together with the new additions, or adds them slowly one at a time to the already well-known song.

We live in a time in which original crafts are being lost. Everything around us is becoming mechanized. The coachman no longer exists, but has been replaced by the mechanic. When a tree needs to be cut down, the lumberjack no longer comes but a man with a howling chainsaw who slaughters the tree. Sometimes a huge machine comes that rips this wonder of nature with root and all out of the ground. Human labor is made mechanical and is dehumanized.

This process cannot be stopped. The only thing we can try to do is channel it. Rudolf Steiner spoke about a time when machines and working with machines will be able to develop in a more moral manner. This future is still far from us. When that time comes, machines will receive a new meaning for young children, but we have not arrived there yet.

We have now arrived in a strange situation. Previously, when work was honest, older school children could start to develop a relationship with its practical sides while the younger ones learned about the crafts through games and songs. Now that mechanization has caused humanity to be less and less involved in this type of work, it is harder and harder to teach the older school children about the practical sides. The younger ones are forced to take school very seriously, leaving little or no time for singing games. These singing games, including the craft games, have now been transferred to the kindergarten years, and communicate their healthy character to the younger children. In this way the "old-fashioned" crafts that used to be practiced by the adult world on a daily basis are kept alive in the form of singing games played in the kindergarten.

Two questions arise. First, how can today's schoolchildren, who are also totally engrossed in modern-day technology, redeem something of the relationship to healthy human physical labor that is so important for their development? And second, what can the old craft games teach children in the kindergarten if they are so old-fashioned? Shouldn't they be replaced by games that will prepare these children for their future?

Regarding the first question, we can say that many schools still give craft and industrial art lessons and many parents sign their children up for arts and crafts classes outside of school. These lessons are important not only because the children learn how to make things, but also because this knowledge has an effect on the rest of their daily lives. Something is picked up and used to fill a void in the soul caused by the mechanization of modern society. Being busy in the creative sense with full enthusiasm and attentiveness "heals" and subconsciously helps to fill this void.

Seen from this point of view, we will be able to understand how important handiwork done by parents and grandparents is for the rest of the family. We have already discussed how deeply a young child is affected by seeing something created out of virtually nothing. If this is done by a trusted parent or grandparent, the effect will be even deeper and an important example is set.

What is the effect on a young child who is not yet ready to participate in this handiwork and only watches? The capacity to participate has not yet woken up in these children, but the foundations for soul content are present and are addressed by the workmanship they see. With repetition, the soul can increasingly identify with the formative activity and find a first entrance to the earthly world, the first subconscious, "dreaming" connection to the new life. We can see this as a type of "birth," a dreaming embodiment of the dormant creative impulses present in the soul. These impulses will become deeds for the first time while playing the craft games.

We will understand that the handiwork made by adults and schoolchildren will not have the same standard as the work of a skilled craftsman. It is not the level of work achieved that is important, but the manner in which the work is done. This is what the children will internalize, and which will become a building stone for their character and their future.

Regarding the second question, we believe that the crafts have only lost their meaning externally, not internally. Their ancient character lives on in our inner being. They have such deeply rooted life and healing forces for humanity in its relationship to the earth that these games can be played through eternity. Hammering and sawing, kneading dough, taking care of others as well as animals—these are basic motifs in human development and are everlasting. For the children they remain a living reality, even if they have never actually seen them being done. The same is true for fairy tales. Most children will never actually see a king in an ermine cape with a gold crown on his head, but this image remains an inner truth. It is an immortal spiritual truth that has found its earthly form in this image. That is what is so important for the children.

Modern technology cannot be shown in a game, but we adults should not turn our back on these new developments, however abstract they may be. We must try to work through these new influences and come out stronger and full of life. However, young children have not yet developed a consciousness for this, and continuous confrontation with such technology will not be entirely favorable for their development. We will have to wait and see which path these new developments will take, hoping that the more and more "mythical" craft games will continue to fulfill their role, much as the king does in fairy tales. And thus we should continue to present the blacksmith, carpenter, baker, lumberjack, washerwoman, farmer, and farmer's wife through the craft games.

But let's not be too rigid with regards to children and modern technology. Children born in modern times are born with new technical knowledge. In their play, they will act out new things such as electricity, washing machines, and the like. This may shock us initially, but if the play is done wholeheartedly, full of free fantasy and joy, there is nothing wrong with it. A plastic car represents a car as much as a wooden one does, even if the material is less "alive." The child experiences this car as a much deeper mode of transportation, as the vehicle that carries our soul through life: our body. I once saw some children pushing cars up a hill of cement and it was as if they were portraying how they must push their own souls up the mountain of life. Aren't telephones and electricity images of connections between souls, a newly acquired community of the soul, and the spreading of light? Even television can be seen in this way. At the moment it is difficult to create games incorporating these machines, but who knows what the future will bring?

I am a blacksmith good and true (for music see page 155)

The next games show a transition from the older to slightly newer game types.[28] The first is the game about the blacksmith, mentioned above. Once again, the children form a circle hand in hand and one child, the blacksmith, stands in the center in front of an anvil but without a hammer. Everyone sings while the smith hammers with his fist on the anvil:

I am a blacksmith good and true,
Best of work I always do.
All day long my hammers go,
Clinging, clinging, clanging so.
A rickety dickety dickety dick,
A rickety dickety dickety dick.

After working the smith calls out to all the children: "Hello, John!" and all the children answer, "Hello, smith!" Smith: "Can you work, John?" Children: "Yes, smith!" Smith: "Can you work with a hammer like me?" Children "Yes, smith!" The song is repeated and the children now hammer in the air together with the smith. The dialogue is repeated, this time ending with "Can you hammer with two hammers like me?" whereupon the children answer "Yes, smith!" and the game is continued while everyone hammers with two hands. Next a foot is added, then two feet, and finally the head (nodding) thus ending with five hammers!

As you will have noticed, this game does not portray the blacksmith's work as such. It is a rhythmical game that portrays the symbolic essence of the craft. The game is played in a *circle*, but its question-and-answer character unmistakably presents something of the *back-and-forth* principle, once again showing a combination of the Father and Son game types. In this game, form and rhythm prevail over the realism of the craft, showing something of its ancient source.

If more realism in this game is wanted, or you are against having the head be used as a hammer (quite harmless, really), then other variations can be thought up, such as "Can you hammer as hard (or soft) as I can?" "Can you hammer as fast (or slow) as I can?" "Can you shoe a horse like me?" "Can you pull on the bellows like me?" All of these movements, although part of the past, are immortal for the young child and can continue to be acted out.

Of course, endless variations are possible for this game. Change blacksmith to farmer, miller, carpenter, nurse, seamstress, cook, and so on. However, always keep in mind what has previously been discussed regarding variations. Once a craft has been chosen and used in all its variations, the song should not be changed.

The Washerwomen (for music see page 156)

The final example of the craft games shows typically female work, even though it is played with as much enthusiasm by boys as by girls: "The Washerwomen." The words are as follows:

> *Come show me your feet, and come show me your shoes,*
> *Let's see what those busy washerwomen do:*
> *They're washing, they're washing, they're washing the whole day through.*
> *They're washing, they're washing, they're washing the whole day through.*

The last two lines are subsequently replaced by:

They're wringing...

They're hanging...

They're ironing...

They're drinking... a cup of tea

They're eating... a piece of cake

They're chatting...

They're dancing...

They're sleeping...

The children stand hand in hand in a circle together with the group leader. There is no child in the center; this is not a question and answer game, and everything is done together. During the first line the children first show one foot to the beat of the music, then the other and tap their toes on the ground. During the second line, they walk around in the circle. With "They're washing, they're washing," they show how they wash in movements. The first two lines are then repeated with the same movements and then the second, "They're wringing, they're wringing," is shown, and so on.

The strange words at the beginning of the song must go back to some forgotten origins. Who would ever have thought up these words nowadays for a song about washerwomen? These can only have come into being over centuries—no logical development could bring such totally unconnected ideas together. But it is this absurdity that frees our thoughts from daily logic so that they are open to experience deeper areas.

We shouldn't ask ourselves what these words *mean* but more importantly what they *do* for the kindergartner. We may then be able to understand how the prelude of showing the feet before walking around addresses the child's deeply anchored will to walk life's path. We must find the transition from trying to understand these symbols to appreciating the child's inner reality.

The beginnings of the will work in the limbs, especially in the legs. Our thoughts only mirror the ideas of the will. The will itself lives in our limbs. These beginnings of the will, which took in impulses before birth and formed them into the tasks and actions to be undertaken in life, and which live with such sparkling force in the young child, are shown through and felt in the limbs. Thus the action of showing the feet is not abstract symbolism for the child.

The biggest task that awaits us in our walk through life is the purification of our soul. Even children are aware of this task, albeit subconsciously. The soul is the cloak of our deepest essence, our "I." It is our silent task to cleanse and refine this cloak during our life on earth. We are the immortal "washerwomen of the soul" going from life to life. Young children have just started a new life, and every time they experience washing, especially washing of clothes, they are silently reminded of this cleansing task. Through the aforementioned game we could say that "walking life's path" and "cleansing the soul" are connected in a playful way.

Craft games are consciously played by the children in mutual agreement, much as work done by adults is done in mutual agreement and with will and feeling. In other words, walking life's path and cleansing the soul are linked to conscious intelligence. We see the three soul functions—willing, feeling and thinking—working together in the games and in reality. We can consciously observe this when watching the children play these games: the children experience this important event in their subconscious where it can continue its work.

The "Washerwomen" game combines these three functions of the human soul on earth. Showing one's feet before starting the journey (walking life's path) reminds us of Rudolf Steiner's statement that it is not only the thoughts in our head but much more the *hidden impulse of the will in our limbs* that takes us on the path through life so that our karma may be fulfilled. Thus the absurd combination of words and actions in the beginning of the song becomes a striking image of the soul life of the child, which originated in the pre-birth soul world.

The connection of these three elements can also be seen in many other games and fairy tales. In "Lay my hankie down" we saw how the soul looked for a good home (cloak) on earth and then suddenly was making a pair of shoes. In "Cinderella" the white (spirit) bird that sits in the tree on her mother's grave gives a clean (soul) cape and a pair of beautiful shoes (again, cloak and shoes) to the girl and these bring her to her prince. And let's not forget how important that one shoe is. Don't children put one shoe by the fireplace on the evening of St. Nicholas so that the holy man can fill it with something for life's path?

The other verses about the daily activities were probably added later. They add a joyful, lighthearted note to the game and should be kept as part of the song, especially for the older children who will understand the fun. The younger ones, who still live in the mystery of everything that they experience in life, will laugh and join the fun imitating the older ones. Their humor has a completely different character, but the general joyfulness will mean something to them.

When looking at this game in its totality, it will have become evident what an important role it plays not only in its typically female character but also in the combination of the three aspects needed to fulfill our earthly life.

Conclusion

We hope that the examples we have chosen to depict the various types of singing games have given a good impression of the nuances that this world of games has to offer. We also hope that we have made the right suggestions in order to be able to adapt the content from its origins to be suitable for children in the kindergarten.

Many leaders who have played and experienced these games with young children may feel encouraged to create games of their own. Even if we only try, the effort will permeate our own being as well as that of the children. Every effort to create something new causes us to grow in our inner being. This growth is experienced by the children in everything that takes place between us and them. We should never give in to an apparent inability to create, but should continue to try, since the rudiments for creation, however unconscious, have been brought with us at birth. Every effort gives this seed the possibility to grow and nurtures the seed present in the children.

Although modern technology doesn't give much material from which to create new games, we should continue to be inspired by the old crafts and trades that still have so much to offer the children. Nothing will give us a better understanding of our relationship to the crafts and to our group of children than trying to create a new game for our own group. However, it is important to mention that the old games should never be replaced by new ones.

In Chapter Six we discussed how self-evident it is that modern humanity cannot create in the same way as our ancient ancestors. For us today, to make a fairy tale in the spirit of the old folk tales or a singing game in the style of the old singing games is relatively or even completely impossible. Anyone who does try to create such a tale or game will undoubtedly be criticized, and be told that it is not filled with the spirit that the old tales and games have. Even if we *were* able to create a tale or game in the spirit of the old ones, we would not have succeeded in fulfilling our task. It is not our task to continue creating in the same manner as before. Modern humanity must develop the ability *to create out of the new, still-developing bond with the spirit*. And with every effort, part of this new bond will be created. Each new bond is the beginning of something new, a seed that must start to grow and find its way in its new surroundings. Anyone who criticizes this new effort, this new seed, and compares it to that what was, blocks, or may even cut off, the way to the future. Every one of us who feels the slightest inclination to start something new, to create a new bond with the spirit, should feel free or should actually feel *obligated* to follow this new road, however difficult it may be. It will be a narrow and twisting road, but it is along this path and not along the wide avenue of the past that we will find the future of mankind, as well as that of the games.

When trying to create a new singing game we will feel that *thinking it through* has little or no value. Take a craft game, for example. In everything that human beings do on earth, thinking is of importance. But the cosmic origins of the craft cannot be found nor shown in thinking. The old craft games let us experience both. In "The Washerwomen," washing, wringing, and ironing are controlled and organized by our "normal" earthly thinking. There is no "normal thinking" that could express the cosmic origins of the will to cleanse on earth, which lives in the limbs and is revealed so clearly by showing the feet. Only ancient humanity's intuition has this power. Since young children still live in this element of intuition, and silently ask us that the singing games approach them within this element, it should be obvious that a new singing game will have to come forth from other powers than just our "normal thinking." Thus we stand before the impossible question of how our limited modern possibilities can let the desired intuitive beginning fulfill its role.

On searching for the right path one thing must always be kept in mind and that is that the children and the world of the games must always be carried in our hearts. Only then will we find inspiration to create something new that will touch the sleeping content that is waiting for our help in the children of our kindergartens. Through this personal endeavor, however primitive or flawed the first efforts may be, the future of singing games that are completely focused on the children themselves will be born.

8 | A healthy awakening from the "childhood dream"

In an earlier book, *Kleuterwereld-Sprookjeswereld* ("The world of the kindergartner—The world of fairy tales," not available in English), we spoke about the fairy tale "The little girl and the toad" by the Brothers Grimm. This fairy tale clearly expresses the essence of the young child (from toddlerhood to kindergarten age) as well as the enormous danger that threatens this phase of life. The fairy tale is about a small girl who befriends a toad. However, the mother thinks the toad is dirty and kills it, after which the child pines away and dies.[29]

At the time it was written this little tale could have been seen as a prophetic warning of the future. This future has now come upon us.

The soul of the young child, which we call the "amphibian" of humanity because it still lingers in the spiritual world while already living in the "dry" earthly world, is represented by the toad. The little girl "becomes friends with the toad." In other words, she carries the essence of the amphibian in her soul, like every young child. The mother represents the sober, levelheaded, thinking adult who doesn't understand this amphibious creature. She kills the "toad" in the girl, thus robbing her of her twofold existence.

When this "toad" within children is killed, they are cut off from their pre-birth spiritual origins. Their cosmic content, the foundation for their later-to-be-searched-for inner development, is therefore also lost, or "dried up." The possibility to achieve an important, if not the most important goal of the life that they have just begun is damaged, or even eliminated. The children's soul content pines away and dies.

Rudolf Steiner has gone so far as to say that the path of a soul that was predestined to live an initiated spiritual life can be diverted or even abolished if it is brought to read and write at an early age. By directing the child's soul to earthly affairs too early, whether physically or psychologically, the bond with the spiritual pre-birth world will be cut off. Of course there are not many souls so great that they are born to lead such a life, but Rudolf Steiner's words let us know how important it is not to awaken children from their "early childhood dream" too early. Every child that is cut off from the spiritual world before it is ready will suffer severe and irreparable damage to the soul.

It is therefore even more important that we learn to see, and maybe even remember from our own experience, how the intense cosmic origins of the child's soul make their way to earthly life through *natural* experiences. This may be through play and fairy tales, or through even earlier experiences (think of the boy and the puddle). If we are aware of the important role these cosmic origins play throughout children's lives, we will understand that we must guard them and nurture the "two-worlds dream" in which they live. We are not just conserving something that is doomed to die. We must allow the cosmic content of the children to find entrance to earthly life *along its own dream path* so that it can accomplish the task that it has been given not only for them, but also for the entire world.

We have already looked at the relationship between the individual and humanity with regard to development. The similarities are immediately evident when we look at the process of development. The young child lives in both the spiritual and earthly world. Humanity did the same in its early development. The expulsion of Adam and Eve from Paradise, as is written in Genesis, can be seen as an image for the whole of humankind who, having allowed themselves to come under the influence of luciferic powers, lost life in the spirit. The descent to life on earth began: a spiritual-earthly occurrence, that in time led to the present earthly life of humanity. During this slow descent, human beings lived in both the spiritual and earthly worlds, something that is clearly seen in the myths and legends passed on through the ages.

The transitional phase went faster for some groups of people than for others and there were many differences. For example, when the Jews had become an earth-aware people, the Germanic and Scandinavian people were still fully connected to their gods, later called angels and archangels. Now, all of modern humanity has descended from the spiritual world, and the direct connection to that world has been lost. But through thousands of years, during the transition from the spiritual to the earthly world, the content of the spiritual world could be experienced when presented in earthly images. The Egyptians spoke of a "soul bird": they experienced the bird as an expression of their soul that was still unconnected to the earthly world. The Greeks talked about Pandora and the gifts given to her by the gods, an image of the spiritually-rich human soul; or Scylla and Charybdis, the two poles of evil between which the sailor (the human soul in life) had to maneuver his boat. The "I" consciousness of the Germanic people on earth grew—Yggdrasil ("carrier of the I")—and they saw the rainbow as a bridge between heaven and earth, between two worlds. Humanity was in its mythical period, in the "two-worlds phase" of its development. The fruits of this period became mythology as we know it today.

What role does mythology play for humanity now? Since myths describe the world of the soul in understandable images, they help us to rediscover the hidden rudiments of spirituality in the earthly world. At first this is only on an intellectual level, but later it will permeate our entire being. Where could mankind possibly begin without these spiritual reminders? We would be like polar explorers who have lost the fuel brought from our homeland, who travel along an ice-cold intellectual path to a deathly cerebral pole. If humanity had not gone through the "two-worlds phase" and did not have spiritual recollections that were immortalized in mythology, we would never be able to rediscover the spiritual world of our origins.

This development is repeated in every one of us. How could adults rediscover the spiritual world in its *living* form if they did not carry the fruits of early childhood experiences within? For children to be able to experience the "spiritual dream" in a healthy and sound way, they must live in balanced and peaceful surroundings. Humanity had a couple of thousand years to experience its "two-worlds phase," but a child has only three or four years—the toddler and kindergarten years.

We must grant a child these years in full. Over-eagerness to reach the next life phase, with haste, disruptiveness, or foreshortening of these years, causes an impoverishment of soul content and thus a violation of all inner developmental possibilities. If the Egyptians and Greeks had been eliminated by some barbaric people, what would this have meant for humanity?

There are two points that we should understand. First, we see how important it is that the spirit be molded into earthly images in order to be carried along in earthly life. This is much like the human soul that must incarnate into a physical body in order to live an earthly life. Each spirit principle must have an earthly "body" in order to travel with us through earthly life. Otherwise it will float away or evaporate. The images we see in fairy tales or games almost never have a transcendental or spiritual character. Hills and valleys, two pairs of shoes, handkerchiefs, and mirrors are all thoroughly earthly objects. They show the children the way *to earth* and give them the possibility to bring rich gifts with them on their way. A traveller who goes through hot deserts cannot bring his water with him in open bowls; it will evaporate in the sun. He can only take it with him in sturdy leather pouches, or earthenware jugs. In the same way, children must be able to "pour" the "spiritual water" into sturdy "jugs" in order to carry it with them through life. Only then will it be able to refresh them during their undoubtedly "spiritually dry" life and give them the necessary life forces out of the spirit.

The second point is the difference between a healthy and unhealthy awakening of the children from their kindergarten dream. If the experiences of early childhood have not been able to develop properly, or if children are woken up too early, they will have extreme difficulty opening to deeper soul content. We could say that the jugs are then "dry," bereft of their spiritual content. Such an awakening would have happened in a sickly, spiritually deprived manner.

A healthy awakening can only occur if children are allowed to experience every aspect of the dream phase needed for their souls to bond with their earthly counterparts. If toddlers have been able to dreamily identify with everything that surrounds them, these things will speak to them by way of their cosmic content. When children in the kindergarten are allowed to play and experience the fairy tales and singing games in a natural and free way, the part of their soul that connects with life in this way will reveal itself to their consciousness at a later stage or live on in their deeper emotions. Then the circle in the game will become the circle of humanity, crafts and labor will have deeper meaning, and the "home of the Father" in fairy tales will be rediscovered in all its spiritual reality. The slow awakening from early childhood will thus play its fundamental role in the deepest levels of the inner development of the child.

It will be obvious that *we* must never awaken a healthy child, however careful we are. It is our task to give children the right environment and content so that they can wake up at their own pace. This content can be found in fairy tales and in the singing games. If we tactfully avoid the dangers mentioned previously in this book and lead the games correctly, they will give much nourishment to the spiritual soul life of the children in the kindergarten. Together with everything else to be experienced in the classroom, they can even help the child recover cosmic origins that may have already been lost. Think, for example, about children who live in modern households, with modern technology and no fairy tales. If they participate in a kindergarten in which fairy tales are told and singing games are played, they are given the possibility to re-experience this phase, a phase which is difficult to experience thoroughly in a modern home. This is another reason why we believe that the kindergarten "classes" are indispensible in modern society.

One thing we must not forget when playing the singing games is that kindergartners are not yet ready to *learn*. This fact should be kept in mind for everything that they are asked to do. Previously, schoolchildren played the games and the little ones looked on and imitated. Almost all new abilities are learned in this way: by watching and imitating. These two things come from within the young child, much more so than in the school-age child, but *we* must give the children this chance. Newcomers to a kindergarten group should be allowed to watch the games played by the older children.[30] In this way they will "imitate within," a hidden process that will surface slowly, allowing the child to eventually join in. This "internal and then external imitation" is the most natural way for newcomers to join the games without the disruptive *learning*.

But is this always possible? What do we do when we introduce a new game? How about if we start a new kindergarten, where essentially *all* the children are new? These are the problems that present themselves through the basic unnaturalness of kindergartens in general, and even more because *school-age* children's games are being played by kindergartners. How can we channel these problems so that a natural solution is found? Since the possibility to watch and imitate is gone in this situation, we will have to find new ways to get the children to join the game.

One possibility is that we begin to hum the song, or sing it softly at a quiet moment during the day. If we repeat this for a number of days, going from humming to softly singing and eventually to adding the words, the children will join in automatically. Then, over time, we can add some movements and finally, when these have also been imitated by the children, we can add the walking element.

We can also approach the game in a different way. We can tell a story in which the content of the game plays a part, for example about a carpenter, or a blacksmith. Then we can slowly add the song and the movements.

It is up to the group leader to find the right way to introduce a new game to his or her group. We must always remember to act with the children in mind, remembering what fits which age group and letting the children remain in their dream worlds.

The final point concerning the singing games is the social element. During the games, we see the children holding each others' hands, listening to each other, letting the other go first, and so on. What does it mean for the kindergartner to *play* such social behavior, especially as it is not yet natural?

The capacity to understand this behavior starts to awaken after approximately the ninth year. Children then start to consciously understand human social behavior that was play-acted in the singing games. However, it is quite different for children in the kindergarten.

The older children in the kindergarten may already have had their first social experience, albeit in a dreaming way. Play-acting this in a game, when done in a light and careful way, may be quite safe and even good for them. For the younger ones (not taking into account the youngest, as they should not be included at all, as discussed earlier) various questions arise. We have seen that we can only understand young children, between toddlerhood and kindergarten age, if we can empathize with the enormous transition they must make from their spiritual origins to their new existence. Since this age group lives so strongly in its pre-birth origins, we can understand that social behavior as we understand it is premature. For example, very young children cannot really "shake hands." If we force them to do this, we will see that they will often extend a fist instead of a flat hand. It is a completely different image: they entrust us with a *fist*, instead of extending a *hand* that exemplifies a warm relationship between equals. Forcing a handshake is unnatural for them and can only cause damage to the pure childlike emotions.

Although it may seem that the intense cosmic soul life and the strong sense life of early childhood stand diametrically opposed to one another, the opposite is true. The strong sense experiences express the children's simultaneously spiritual and earthly life. They rediscover the one in the other through the senses. In a larger context we could say: the human soul comes to earth primarily to observe how the earthly world reveals the spirit. This is what young children do inwardly, sometimes in a very lively and "awake" way so that it almost seems that it is not a "dreaming experience." However, on the inside they experience the unification of the cosmos and earth in a deep "dreaming" state. It is through this knowledge, not a superficial interest, that the children use their senses so intensely and so fully. For them, the senses unify the two worlds.

How could young children, who experience everything so intensely through the senses, be able to be social, as we understand it? Human relations are no less important than the spiritual world, but these move on such different levels that to unify them is virtually impossible for this age group. If we *do* demand this from children, we will undoubtedly disrupt the transition they are undergoing.

This is different when we look at the games. Here the social element is not asked of the child *personally*. It is *played together*. Thus it does not awaken consciousness. Young children cannot put themselves in the position of another out of "courtesy," but they can understand the social elements played in a game from a *cosmic perspective*. When forming an arch for another child to pass through, they will not do this out of courtesy for the other child, but in recognition of their own souls passing through an archway on their way to earth. If we make sure that the younger children can play along or watch the others play this game, they will subconsciously understand these social elements and eventually be able to incorporate them into their own lives.

Not being able to be social is not a matter of being ego-centric but of being "cosmo-centric." Children whose souls are still carried and enveloped by their spiritual origins can only search for the earthly world out of that world, and then only for themselves. Put into the words of spiritual science: the children still live in the world of the Father and find this world in their new earthly environment. They are led by the Son but cannot yet express or look for the forces of the Son. That is why *active* social human relations are still out of the question.

When working with children we cannot possibly keep all these points in mind. We must do as much as the given situation allows us to do. The most important thing is that we have a feeling for what is happening in the children and can act accordingly. Only then can the right consciousness develop and grow.

Adults who cannot see, or experience for themselves, that children live in these two worlds will find it difficult to understand that this is the basis for children's inner development. They will think that our concern is misplaced or exaggerated. It is possible that they will applaud the general push to hasten the development of a child and welcome the superficial results. The hidden possibilities for the future that are thus destroyed in the child will be meaningless for them. What they see as nervousness, one-sidedness, or impoverishment of soul life will not be attributed to superficiality or the accelerated pace of life. It is not generally understood that human beings differentiate themselves from the animals in that they have a personal, peaceful, and slow development. Instead, animal qualities such as speed and sharpness are the motto of modern life.

Thus it will be understandable that adults must first rediscover something of their *own* spiritual origins before they will be able to understand what the children have brought with them. Only then will this richness be seen consciously as a healthy breeding ground for inner development. Only then can the necessity of the *human slow awakening* of the childlike soul from its cosmic origins to the earthly world, to which each soul brings its content and gifts, be experienced. This may only be a dream for the future, but we must do our best to start the process.

In everything we have talked about until now, we have always had a *healthy* child in mind. As soon as there is a different balance, everything changes. If a child has a disease of some sort, it may be necessary to stimulate the awakening process through medicine or other measures. A person who is under anesthesia must be woken up slowly, carefully. However, if someone is in a healthy sleep his soul is helped by leading forces and circumstances and will find the right way and the right time to wake up. Healthy sleep is followed by healthy awakening that can only be determined by the relationships among the forces in the spiritual world. Any earthly interference with this process is *un*healthy. The same is true for the greater awakening of the child's soul.

We have spoken about how each child must find the right individual and personal way to awaken from the childhood dream. We adults can help the children by giving them the right environment and circumstances. This can be seen as contrary to the practical and perhaps one-sided opinion that our primary goal should be to prepare the child for the modern world. This is the world in which they will have to live. Procrustes from Greek mythology now comes to mind.[31] Aren't we trying to make the child's soul "fit" modern life, as Procrustes did with the limbs?

Obviously, we should allow the children to find their way in the modern world. Let's not be unrealistic. But we should not forget that what needs to be adapted or healed is not the child's soul but the modern world. If the modern world is adapted to the child, it can begin to heal. We as adults must lead this healing process and help the children bring their deepest content and gifts to their new existence, not only for themselves, but for the entire world. Thus we will understand how important it is that we appreciate what each child brings.

We should also look at the temperaments with regard to waking up out of the "cosmic dream." We may be inclined to see the quick and "awake" actions and reactions of the sanguine child, or the slowness of the phlegmatic child, as a mirror for the way their souls descend to earth. The boldness of the choleric or the moodiness of the melancholic child might seem to show us their different deep inner longing for the earthly world.

The reality is quite different. The temperament lies in the physical-etheric *shell* that surrounds the soul. Awakening out of the spiritual dream is a *process* that is experienced and accomplished in its deepest sense by the child. The enormous difference lies in the fact that we should only watch over and care for the deep process of awakening, while the temperament, as shell of the soul, should be harmonized during life and thus should be worked on and revised.

Adults should work on their own temperaments individually, but obviously children must be helped and led by us. A child's temperament begins to be seen most clearly after the teeth start changing, which is after the kindergarten years. When we are confronted with the question of whether the actions of a child should be seen as an expression of his "I," his deepest essence, or of his temperament, we should look closely at his eyes. What we called the young child's "Janus-look," looking inward and outward at the same time, can be seen as the most telling sign of the actions coming from his hidden deepest essence. If we experience this "Janus-look" frequently, it can become a silent schooling for us that may open the deepest inner path to the cosmic depths of the child and of ourselves.

The enormous meaning behind the long childhood dream can also be seen from a different angle. When we ask ourselves which fairy-tale characters are the ones who turn out to be the best or most important, aren't these mostly the characters that started out as seeming to be the least intelligent, or most neglected?[32] It seems that the most important characters in the world of fairy tales are the ones whose hidden spiritual content did not fit earthly spheres initially, but who could in the end accomplish their tasks.[33]

In the French tale "Puss in Boots," the young, stupid miller's son, who is only good enough to inherit a cat (that is, the one who inherits the least and thus has the most of himself), in the end marries the king's daughter. In the Grimms' fairy tale "Cinderella"[34] it is the stepsister who is good for nothing except to do the dirty housework. In the end she marries the prince and (outside of the tale) becomes queen.[35]

In order to understand what is the opposite of healthy awakening, we could sketch a picture of what would have happened to the miller's son had he been "healed" from his stupidity, that is, been robbed of his slow awakening. What would have happened if he had inherited more than just the cat and went through life, or rather, *had* to go through life, as a "normal," intelligent person? What would have happened to Cinderella had she been more aware and able to stand up to her stepsisters, and had entered the ballroom in the same way as they did? In the first story the role of the wise cat would have been nullified. In the second, the tree and the mother from the spiritual world would not have been able to fulfill their roles. Both fairy tales would have become meaningless and the characters would not have been able to find their true paths in life and fulfill their given tasks. The fairy tales show us our responsibility with regard to the slow awakening of young children so that they can find their way in life and later fulfill the task that has been given to them.

Unfortunately, the modern world almost always sees the "awakened brothers" as the ones who are on the correct path and takes them as a role model for the slower dreamers. Fairy tales, in their ancient wisdom, tell us that this is not the case. When playing the singing games, which were originally created by and for school-age children, we must be careful to choose the slowest, least hurried games, those that fit the group and each child individually.[36] An undertaking on its own!

In our time there is an urge to modernize. People are looking for new paths everywhere, in the arts, religion, pedagogy. However, a hidden but increasingly pressing issue is the need to rediscover the lost soul content of mankind and the world (expressed in the word "religion," which is possibly derived from Latin *re-ligare*, to reconnect). In our opinion this seems to still play a very minor role. The old principles, which often still carried something of what was lost but which cannot keep up with the new times, are discarded. Our foundation no longer lives in that which is put in its place. The dominant urge is external rationality, causing the past to be lost. At the same time, we are not yet consciously looking for the deeper meaning of what the future wants from us. It is possible that this is a transition phase, but the danger exists that we will become more and more estranged from our soul content as well as our soul future, causing us to become more and more materialistic.

The same is true when looking at the upbringing of young children. The old is discarded but there is no real replacement that is focused on the future. The focus is on the external, materialistic side, which can be totally misleading when searching for the true possibilities of the child. The most important question for us is: how can we help young children find the correct path through this life, while keeping their cosmic, pre-birth content intact? If we do not address this question, the children will be damaged. Doing away with fairy tales because they "do not tell the truth" and teaching kindergartners to read and write so that they get a head start on their development are all reforms in education, even though they originated in the beginning of the twentieth century. That these reforms have an extremely unfavorable effect on the inner development of the young child is unknown or forgotten.

All of the above tells us how important it is that we *consciously* aim to have the right relationship with that which children have brought with them from the cosmos. We must learn to sympathize with that part of the children that makes up their deepest origins, the most vulnerable part. We must develop a living understanding of the soul content of children, without which they can be drastically damaged, leading to disturbances in the soul whose origins cannot be found. We are given the not-so-simple task of finding, or re-discovering, the cosmic origins of the child, which are after all our own origins.

How does the development of humanity relate to the origins of our soul? The original connection between humanity and the spiritual world could not continue on its own. According to the larger world plan, this connection had to diminish so that we would slowly recover it out of our yet-to-be-acquired personal independence. We could not start on this long road toward developing independence without the help of the spiritual world. In ancient times, this help came by way of the mysteries, through which spiritual initiates kept a certain connection with the supernatural world, laying the foundations for freedom of thought. In the time of the Mystery of Golgotha, the old mysteries came to an end and spiritual leadership was taken over by the church. The church, with all its dogmas and theories, had to lead people who had already lost much of their spiritual origins and who had not yet found their own spiritual path. These church leaders were able to develop in their own way, but in general humanity remained far removed from its spiritual origins and became increasingly materialistic.

Nevertheless, a hopeful phenomenon did arise. Although most people rejected spirituality, there were some who began to look for the cosmic element in life. They were like seedlings for mankind's future soul life. In the eighteenth and nineteenth centuries movements led by people such as Schiller and Goethe appeared. It was in the beginning of the twentieth century that the spiritual world itself sent support and help from which this free and independent search for the spiritual in general could grow. This help came in the form of Rudolf Steiner's spiritual science, through which anyone can look for the spirit in his or her *own, personal* way.

However, with this development opposite forces also surfaced. Rudolf Steiner foresaw a radical struggle at the end of the twentieth century between the forces of light (of the spirit) and the dark forces. The outcome of this struggle would determine the further development and possibilities of mankind on earth. A second movement would arise that would show the spiritual impulses on an artistic, religious level. According to anthroposophy, a worthy progression and a full development of humanity will only be possible if these two movements work together and are unified.

Rudolf Steiner tells us that the origins of this spiritual movement can be found in the ancient Greeks. Here he mentions our extremely influential predecessors Aristotle (the sciences) and Plato (arts and religion).[37]

At the end of this the twentieth[38] and the beginning of the twenty-first century the souls belonging to the Platonic movement—the Aristotelian forces have already begun—will have an important role to fulfill. These souls, which have wonderful gifts from the spiritual world to give to the earth, will need an exceptionally slow awakening from their childhood dream in order to allow their soul content to be incarnated without being damaged. This slow awakening is essential for them to be able to realize that which they have been born to do. Thus, if we speak in fairy-tale terms, in their childhood they will belong to the "stupid youngest brothers and sisters."

This means that these souls will be among us as young adults at the end of the twentieth century. What an enormous responsibility for us adults to recognize and accompany these rich souls in their slow awakening, for the sake of themselves and the rest of the world!

May it grow to be a deeply conscious assignment for all who can develop such a consciousness to give these unusual (but harmonious and healthy) "youngest brothers and sisters" the possibility to cultivate their childhood dream quietly and in their *own* time. Of course, there will not be many parents chosen to accompany such an important soul from the Platonic movement, but *all* people can contribute to the growth of such a universal consciousness and to improving the circumstances of young children. Both tasks will be indispensible for what is meant to be developed in the future. Thus we should *all* feel a subtle responsibility for the just development of these events, and for everything that will be accomplished through them.

9 Rhythm and ritual: The possible origins of singing games

What role does the element of rhythm have in various religions? When thinking about this question, primitive dances meant to ward off sickness or bring extra power before a war expedition may come to mind. Such dances may be decadent, wild, maybe even evil, full of black magic. And then, if we ask ourselves what the element of rhythm plays in Christian services, we may become puzzled.

As we saw earlier, rhythm can work in many different ways and plays a fundamental role in our lives. In Christianity it plays a subtle, but at the same time very active and important role. However, if misused, anything that is important or uplifting can tip over and descend to the lowest level. There is a saying, "From the elevated to the absurd is only one step." We could add that this one step could be the step to the dark side. If we use God's name in vain, it becomes a curse. We have already seen that healthy rhythm works in an opposite way if a small child is woken up to active rhythm too early. In the same way active, enthusiastic rhythm can take on a negative character even though its true form is uplifting.

What would the world be without the divine foundations of rhythm? The world is built on rhythm: the movement of the sun, the tides, the seasons, human life with its pulsing circulation. This pulse beats through everything that is alive and in development. This is the true essence of rhythm, which fulfills its role in everything that can develop physically or spiritually. From these foundations it can achieve the highest, most hidden point in which the divine lives: Christ. It is Christ who lives in *good* rhythm. Rudolf Steiner puts this into words in his Foundation Stone Meditation: *Denn es waltet der*

Christuswille im Umkreis in den Weltenrhythmen seelenbegnadend. "For the Christ Will in the encircling round holds sway, in rhythms of Worlds bestowing grace upon souls."

If we agree with the above, how could Christianity without rhythm truly be part of the spirit of Christ? Wouldn't Christianity then be a one-sided, theoretical, abstract "belief" rather than a living creed? Our physical body cannot live without the rhythms of heartbeat and breathing, nor can our soul be part of the spirit without this essential element.

In reality Christianity is imbued with rhythm. Sunday, with its church services, has a special meaning. In the services themselves we see that the Catholic Mass and the Act of Consecration of Man of the Christian Community are filled with rhythm that is alive. In the latter we feel that the mindset of the priest and the congregation with regard to Christ is an alternation between silently receiving and in a certain sense actively giving, between prayer and offering. The entire world of the Christian Community is built around a larger rhythm, that of the seasons and the annual Christian festivities.[39]

It has been said that something great happened on the last evening of Christ's life, a "once-only mystery circle game" or a "once-only ritual dance." There is an apocryphal story[40] that says that on the last evening Christ asked his apostles to form a circle hand in hand. He stood in the center and said: "Answer me every time by saying Amen." Then he said or chanted the words of a hymn: "Praise be to you, Father." John the Evangelist tells us further: "And we walked in a circle and answered Amen! . . 'Praise be to you, Logos!' . . . Amen! 'Praise be to you Spirit, Holy Spirit'. . . Amen!" After the hymn, Christ said, "Those who do not join in this game, are not part of me," a statement that could also pertain to *us*.

Let's look at what Rudolf Steiner said in a lecture[41] about the ancient midsummer festival of western Europe. He describes how initiates brought the people who still lived in their cosmic consciousness, especially those living in those regions, to celebrate when the sun stood at its highest. During these celebrations they sang, played music on primitive instruments, and danced rhythmical ritual dances. The higher "I" of humanity, which still lingered in the cosmos, was temporarily brought down to earth during this ritual of rhythmical music, song, and dance. The "I"-being of these people was briefly absorbed by their dream consciousness. They experienced their individuality subconsciously as a preparation for the necessary "I"-conscious life of humanity's future on earth.

Rudolf Steiner also tells us that these people, when they were completely absorbed in music and song, felt like singing birds—not only because they were completely absorbed in singing, but also because of the echo that came from the cosmos. This echo was like a blessing sprinkled over the "birdsong," the human song and the ritual dance. Steiner tells us that when a bird sings, his song is received in the cosmos and arouses an "echo" that returns to the bird world and the entire animal world as a blessing. Something like this happened for human beings during these midsummer rituals. After having played their music and danced, the people were brought to a listening state by the initiates so that they would be able to receive this blessing. They became "listeners" to what came as a divine answer to their song and dance. Much like water that evaporates, returns to the heavens to become clouds, and then falls as rain that enriches the earth, in the same way the singing and dancing was lifted up to the heavens and came back as a divine blessing. During this *inner* listening, the subconscious "I"-experience came to them.

The human "Amen" could be experienced as the "echo" to the Christ hymns of the ritual dances as described in the apocryphal story above. They can be experienced as a "response phenomenon" of the three larger echoes that come to us from the Foundation Stone Meditation,[42] those of the Father, the Son, and the Holy Spirit.

In the first part of the meditation, which is dedicated to the Father-God, we hear:

> *Lasset aus den Höhen erklingen,*
> *Was in den Tiefen das Echo findet.*
>
> *Let there ring out from the heights*
> *What in the depths finds its echo.*

These words, which are directed to the highest beings of the hierarchies, ask that an echo may be found in the depths of the earthly world to the sounds coming from the spiritual world. This relationship between God and human beings, heaven and earth, is what this first part of the meditation speaks of.

In the second part, dedicated to the Son, we hear:

Lasset vom Osten befeuern,
Was durch den Westen sich formet.

Let from the East be enkindled
What through the West takes on form.

This part is directed to the second hierarchy, where the sun rises, in the East. This provides warmth, or "enthusiasm" for the impetus of the spirit that must find its solid form in the West, a process that currently moves across the earth, coming from the East and finding solid ground in the West.

The third part, that of the Spirit, tells us:

Lasset aus den Tiefen erbitten,
Was in den Höhen erhöret wird.

Let from the depths be entreated
What in the heights will be heard.

Once again a relationship between heaven and earth, this time reversed when compared to the part dedicated to the Father: earth to heaven instead of heaven to earth.

This part is directed to the third hierarchy: what mankind, from the depths of the earth, asks for and is heard in the heavens: a plea that human spiritual life will find its echo in heaven.

Thus we have three "echoes." The first, speaking in practical terms, "vertical," the second "horizontal" and the third once again "vertical" but reversed.

The echo phenomena that we have talked about—in the ritual dance of Christ with the apostles, in the midsummer festival, and the trilogy of echoes in the Foundation Stone Meditation—should now be seen in a wider context in order to understand more about the origins and the meaning of children's games.

The first question that arises is why a midsummer and not a midwinter festival was spoken of. After all, nowadays we are more focused on the elements of the earth that allow us to find our most wakeful "I"-consciousness in winter.[43] The answer that we will try to give below may also shed more light on the development of the young child and the meaning of early childhood.

In the past, the true, higher "I" was revealed subconsciously. Today, it is hidden almost entirely and spiritual development takes place by means of *thought* of the *everyday*, or lower "I." *This* spiritual development is best done in the wakefulness of winter. However, while consciously *thinking*, we must try to raise ourselves to the domain of the higher "I." This is a task that we must see as fundamental for spiritual development *in our time*.

Ancient humanity could not accomplish this task: it could not even exist as such. How could human beings rediscover the higher consciousness that they still partly had, if they had not yet descended? The task for humanity at that time was to find earthly science and logic in thought and consciousness, from which elevation would be possible. Descending to the earthly world mostly happened during the winter. But in order to carry the cosmic content that resided in higher worlds, even in hidden form, cosmic origins had to be re-experienced. And that could only happen in the summer. While singing and dancing, at the same time as nature itself was rising to the heavens, and listening to the spiritual echo, human beings could experience something of the higher "I" and implement it in their increasingly earthly existence. In a way these experiences went "underground." They could then be transported into the future as seeds from which the higher "I" could grow more conscious and develop to larger proportions on earth.

This development could be seen as a parallel movement to the old myths and legends of ancient humanity. Of the images that were previously mentioned, the one that comes to mind is "Yggdrasil" ("I"-carrier), the tree whose immense trunk and crown reaching to the heavens allowed the "I" in its earthly form to be experienced. This image enabled human beings to subconsciously carry much of their hidden spiritual foundations with them on the descent to earthly existence, so that these foundations were kept alive. Up to a certain point these mythical images can fulfill the same role for modern humanity: they also give us something of the "dreaming possibility of descent." However, recognition for us lies more in *understanding* the images in order to rediscover something of our cosmic origins. We can then consciously undergo something of the ascending development.

In young children, we can see parallels with ancient humanity: children also have a completely "summer" character in the early years. In other words, young children experience their inner development (or "echoes") dreamily or subconsciously, without wakeful understanding, even if they are completely awake and physically lively. Much as humanity had a "listening" experience after ritual dances and a dreaming "recognition" of mythical images and the world, the children in the kindergarten have their dream experiences with regard to their surroundings, especially in play and toys, in picture books, fairy tales, and singing games. Their development is a "dreaming descent," not a "conscious ascent" of the soul. Hidden in the images of the world and the image experiences of the soul, the unborn "I" can subconsciously enter earthly life. From here, after having achieved full, wakeful, earthly consciousness, the "I" will begin the search for the world of the spirit.

The environment that we create in the kindergarten can easily be compared to what previously was brought to still-dreaming humanity in early times through the midsummer festival, as well as through the tales told in myths. These gifts of song, music, dance, and story, and the inner development that they brought about, are very close to the games, songs, and fairy tales given to and experienced by the kindergartners. The children, in their "two worlds" reality, certainly resemble early humanity, which still felt and experienced its higher cosmic origins subconsciously.

But what is the role of the group leader? How do we see *her* in the middle of all of this? Do we dare to put her in the same context as the initiates of the midsummer festivals, whose task it was to help mankind find its way to earthly existence? A smile will undoubtedly come to many a leader's face when thinking about this. They will immediately understand the great differences, especially on the level of soul consciousness. Nevertheless, the similarities are striking.

After hearing of Rudolf Steiner's explanation of the Western European pre-Christian midsummer festival ritual dances, the ritual dance that Christ performed with his followers will undoubtedly strike us even more. We can join Dr. Jurriaanse (see note 40) in assuming that this dance around Christ can be seen as a fulfillment of the earlier ritual dances, during which the initiates had the people walk around and sing, then stand and listen to the higher "I"-consciousness that still lived in the cosmos (in other words, the "I" that still lived in Christ). Christ, who had not yet appeared on earth and was unknown to non-initiates, was therefore the true center. Later, when He danced with the apostles, he was the true center on earth. The apostles, who, like early humanity, experienced their "I" in Christ, could now do this with a measure of earthly consciousness. For the first time *directly on earth* mankind, represented by the apostles, could receive the blessing from the Lord himself to wake up to a higher level in their own "I." They could wake up in their own deeper humanity.

If we compare this first step taken by humanity to the Foundation Stone Meditation, we can see the transition from the first to the second "echo." The earliest ritual dances let us experience the first: the "heaven-earth echo," the Father-forces through which human beings felt carried and sheltered in the religious circle. However, the Son was the invisible center of this "Fatherly-human circle." It was this invisible presence that realized on an earthly level in later ritual dances, when Christ was physically present. Only then could the second echo, the "horizontal echo," in which Christ and his followers speak and answer, sing and are sung to, be realized *on earth*.

What emanated from Christ to his followers, what inspired them and therefore made them representatives for all of humanity, could be awakened by their "human thankfulness" and "human prayers" and, in their "amen," be directed back to Him. The "back-and-forth principle" played out in the singing games is the beginning of the larger reality that can be found in the second part of the Meditation called "rhythms of Worlds," in which the "Christ-will bestows grace upon souls."

Where can we find the third echo of this Meditation, the heavenly echo to the question that is spiritually raised out of earthly conditions? Where can we find what is meant in the words, "Let from the depths be entreated, what in the heights will be heard"?

After the time during which God came to Abraham, when Moses received the Ten Commandments from Jehovah, when the prophets lived directly under the influence of the spiritual world, came the time when Christ lived on earth among human beings. The Petrine Christianity of the Church spread from East to West and found solid ground in the West. But a Christianity in which humanity looks for Christ as a full spiritual reality *out of themselves* and out of their *earthly life* was yet to come. The first seeds of this Christianity came from the apostle who "would wait": John. They began their first, slow germination during the events that the apostles experienced at Pentecost. Only in the twentieth century, though, have we begun to ask ourselves whether the possibility to search for ourselves has been granted. Isn't it true that we have been given the insights and impulses that would make such a development possible? Don't we understand through these insights that the question is not of a "new religion" but a "new road"; a road that we will have to create ourselves out of our own lives, out of our own thoughts that are reaching toward what the future asks from us?

Jehovah no longer speaks to us—or rather, we no longer hear Him speaking. No ritual dances around our Savior, no religion, can create a new world, but we have been shown the *way* of the spirit. The question now is to what extent this way is recognized: was it understood in the past, is it recognized in the present, and will it be searched for in the future? As young children, like ancient humanity, we began by dreamily experiencing the Father-world in our souls. Then, like the people of the Middle Ages, we heard the sounding of what lives and winds its way between people, back-and-forth, the deeper essence of which is carried by the strength of the Son. Now, as adults of our time, we will have to *re*-discover the spiritual world from the earthly depths in which we now find ourselves. We hope that once all three echoes are active together, earthly life in its full essence, in honest human relationships, will be able to develop to its true spiritual height.

Let's turn back to the children. In young children the three soul echoes that we spoke about are felt quite differently than in modern adults and will thus have to be led differently. What we previously called the "dreaming recognition experience" of early childhood can be seen as the "echoes" of childish soul life. Remember how real the cosmic origins of the element of *water* feel for young children, and how they re-experience their own cosmic soul content in this element. They experience their own content as "echoes" in the water and can be completely taken in by this "echo experience" in everything that is water. In the same way, we can see how young children experience everything around them as an "echo" of their own cosmic soul content. We also feel how firmly they must live in the first echo, the Father echo, in order to find entrance to the earthly world. This is the reason that the Father-character is of primary importance in the circle games that we sing and play in the kindergarten.

When we start the back-and-forth games with the older children, we will discover that the "horizontal echo" is experienced quite differently by the children than by us, especially when playing these games with an adult. If the "question and answer" is played across from an adult, the children will experience this strongly as being *carried* by the adult (the Father). It is only between the children themselves that the rudiments of question and answer can begin to be experienced "horizontally." However, we should also understand that the entire field of the second echo is relative for young children and is mostly experienced in the realm of the Father.

How about the third echo, the echo that rises up, the echo in the heavens of our search for the higher powers of the spirit? It will be obvious that an ascending search was not possible at the same time that mankind was descending to earth. Likewise, for the children this is a deeply slumbering future. It therefore also follows that an upward surge (including its echo) should be kept hidden from the child in the singing games. But we don't have to worry about this, for in the games this echo is only implied. In a previous chapter we spoke about "going down the path of development together" as represented in the line games. For the children in the kindergarten, who are not yet ready for this united spiritual path, walking together in a line will only be experienced as "going through life together." The youngest ones will not even be able to experience it as such since they are not yet ready for this aspect in their development. They are still "individualists" on their *own* path.

The line game also takes the children through an arch, a "gateway" that we should see as a "spiritual gateway." Fairy tales tell of a beautiful world that opens to us when we pass under this arch. This is not the case in the games. The children will more likely feel themselves directed more to earth when passing under the arch than to higher worlds. As the game is played together, they will probably also feel more connected to the other children.

Through these examples it should be obvious that the rudiments of the third echo play only a very minor role in the singing games as well as in all the experiences of the children. We can imagine that this ascending echo principle was hardly present during the midsummer festivities and thus understand that it is also not yet consciously present in young children. The feeling that *is* experienced in a line game, though extremely far off, may be felt again and understood when the child reaches adulthood, and then developed further.

Of all the echo experiences of the small child we should learn to feel the importance of the strongly present first echo, the Father echo. If we understand the meaning, we will be able to let it do its important work.

Everything that we have read and heard about ancient singing games and ritual dances leads us to ask: to what extent we can see these past events as the foundations of modern singing games for children? Of course the first thought that will come to mind is the similarity to the first circle dance in Palestine. Even the mixture of the circle and back-and-forth element is often seen in our present circle games. However, the most important aspect—that of Christ himself in the middle of the circle of apostles, the epitome of human relationships, who at the same time was the "Father" for his sons—was not possible anywhere else, nor could it ever be possible again. It happened on the evening before an event that could only happen once, the crucifixion. We will have to accept that nothing could directly follow what was accomplished between Christ and his apostles. It has only continued and still continues in hidden form in the development of humanity.

How different it must have been during the pre-Christian summer feasts that were repeated annually for years, probably centuries, when the sun stood at its highest point. These rituals were widespread, according to Rudolf Steiner. One of their most important roles was to prepare for the coming of Christ on earth, although we can imagine that they also took place after His coming. First of all, it took Christianity quite some time to penetrate to all corners of the earth. And then, even when these areas had accepted Christianity, the task thus being fulfilled, the rituals were often maintained. We often see rituals of old beliefs penetrate a new religion, albeit in somewhat altered form.[44]

In the abovementioned case we can imagine that it was the initiates who slowly withdrew from the festivities as they saw that their task was completed. Other people, especially the younger ones, who enjoyed the festivities the most, continued the celebrations. Thus the leaders changed from initiates to non-initiates, and the festivities came to be carried by tradition rather than from their spiritual essence. As human beings gradually lost more and more cosmic soul life, participation in the summer celebrations would eventually not have been felt as a natural part of the year anymore, and would have been kept alive by younger generations, eventually to be left to children in whom spirituality still found a foundation. The games would also not only have been played in summer but throughout the year, and the lyrics, form and movements would have changed until they became what we now know as the singing games of children.

In this way—somewhat freely but still keeping to well-known facts—we have attempted to create an idea of the origins of the singing games, an attempt that may be just as freely continued, changed, or discarded by readers. The older generation among us experienced the last step of the games: bringing them from school-age children into the kindergarten. As we have seen, this step must still be made to become a true and healthy reality. We have now also come to the outermost edge of the rejuvenation, since allowing children younger than kindergarten age to participate is damaging to their health however much the games are adapted. For toddlers there are lap games that *we* play *with* them, and that are indispensable for them.

For the children, the singing games and the entire kindergarten itself can be seen as a certain repetition in miniature of what came to pre-Christian people through the mysteries, when initiates gave still-dream-conscious human beings the chance to enter the earthly world while retaining their larger cosmic content. Thus they could later rediscover the spiritual world on earth in accordance to what Christ would give them. In much the same way, we adults, as parents and kindergarten leaders, must give young children the chance to incarnate. The kindergarten leader, who leads the singing games in full consciousness of all that we have considered above, can be seen as a successor to the initiated leaders of the pre-Christian midsummer rituals.

If they are able to lead the singing games in such a way that they genuinely help the children find their way to earth, group leaders will be a part of the "descent" through their actions. They will help to make the kindergarten experience a significant and spiritual reality.

10 The task of the early childhood group leader today

Today's kindergarten leaders have an immensely varied task, and those who lead groups for even younger children have a task that is even more new and unprecedented. Both roles have become indispensable in modern society for the healthy development of young children, and both originated through developments that can be viewed with a certain sadness. A century ago, almost all kindergartners (and certainly toddlers) were at home with their mothers. They saw everything that Mother did in the home, they saw Father leave for work in the field or elsewhere, and now and again an older brother or sister played with them. They then made a kite, or a doll, and the little ones watched while the older children played circle games or other games with children from the neighborhood. If we go back another hundred years or so, we come to the times of the legendary grandmothers who told fairy tales to grandchildren while sitting around the fireplace. Most likely little friends from the neighborhood also came to listen to the sound of Grandmother's voice.

"What a paradise for the young child!" we may think, looking back with nostalgia. But that feeling gets us nowhere. Yes, we should remember the old times, but we should not lose ourselves in them. The good old times will not return, although we must be aware the past in order to be able to turn to the future. We should try to create "good new times" full of our love and understanding for the young child, and also full of understanding of our modern age.

The care that we give to reaching this goal lies between the poles of *protecting* and *giving*. Protectively, we must devote our care to the cosmic content that still lives in the children's souls and is searching for a way to earthly life. We must safeguard these valuable possessions of the children against the harmful influences that they may come across in the modern world—for example, school learning that they pick up along the way at the expense of their cosmic core, or the influence of too much radio or television. There is much that we should guard against in modern society.

There is another activity that lies between protecting and giving. We will certainly encounter situations in which harmful elements have already found an entrance into the life of the children and we cannot eliminate them anymore. It is then up to us to use our pedagogical imagination and try to *bend these elements away* from what is harmful so that they become positive and meaningful. The letters that some children may have learned can be changed into pictures with a story attached, so that the children's imagination is brought to life. This story can grow or be repeated at will. Watching television can be diminished by spending more time looking at picture books together and making up stories to go with the pictures.

We can review daily life with the child: caring for a younger brother or sister, cooking, cleaning, parents going to work, children playing. We may also bring the children's attention to what is happening outside: a bird rummaging around in the garden, looking for food or twigs to build a nest. All in all, there are enough things that we can show or do that are important for the *inner life* of the child. In this way much of what has been damaged can be repaired and changed.

Regarding the pole of *giving*, we should try to give the children what is good for them *directly*. We can let toddlers play in water, let them lose themselves in the "fluidity" of sand, or give them anything else that lets them encounter their cosmic heritage through earthly matter. We can take them on our laps and sing lap songs or play lap games that are profoundly valuable. Kindergartners can be progressively introduced to fairy tales, allowed to draw and color, given sturdy and healthy toys, and so on.

How do we place the kindergarten leaders and children of today in a modern context? It's hard not to see the classes and their leaders as a "forced novelty" as compared to the bygone ideal described above. Instead of the toddlers being watched over by Mother, the kindergartners being told fairy tales by the fireplace by Grandmother, and the slightly older children watching Father working at his craft, we have taken the children out of their natural family context and put them into various groups. Mother and grandmother have been replaced by an appointed group leader, who will have had to study hard and earn a degree to be able to be a "surrogate mother" for the children.

It is obvious that kindergarten group leaders must have studied a great deal and must also have a natural feeling for young children. Otherwise they would never have chosen this job. But there will usually be an important aspect missing from what they have learned. That is their natural, if generally still hidden, feeling for the cosmic origins of the essence of the child. This is not taught in teacher training courses, but in our view it should be the foundation for working with and caring for young children. It is therefore extremely important that the leaders work at the task of searching for these cosmic origins. Only then can they *consciously* protect the children from what may hurt or damage them. Only then can the children experience a quiet and calm soul awakening so that the cosmic content that they must bring to earth can develop further and enrich the rest of their lives.

In order to be able to lead schoolchildren, teachers must understand the social background of each child. In order to truly take care of toddlers and kindergartners, the group leaders must not only know the social background, but also the larger context from which the *souls* of the children have come. If leaders experience empathizing with the pre-birth "soul environment" of the children as a leitmotif in their work, this will contribute to a deeper realization of their task. Then they will be able to counter the artificiality of starting "classes" at this age, and turn their kindergartens into *new*, healthy experiences.

Many parents, in spite of modern influences, will do their best to lead their children according to the ways we have described in this book. But this does not have to be limited to parents. We adults will have to cultivate a general consciousness of what is good for children, so that the entire threatened world can benefit from what today's young children bring with them from the cosmic Father-realm. Many of us will want to contribute to this development.

If group leaders, when doing their profound work, can create an inner openness for the cosmic origins of the young child, they will be able to lead the children's souls along the right path in their new life, and will then be able to safeguard these souls from the aggressions of the modern world. These aggressions don't eliminate cosmic life itself, but they close the door to this life. At the same time, such leaders will be able to connect to the cosmic content of the child as a foundation and source for further inner development.

If some group leaders cannot bring themselves to "listen" to the inner, hidden life of the children that wants to communicate with us, we must still value the love and devotion they bring to caring for the children, and should still be happy with the results. It would be even more tragic if these children were to become estranged from their true, early experiences by being surrounded by unnaturally happy and jovial adults. They would be like people robbed of their essence, even though they received love and attention, and many of them would have to go through life without ever rediscovering anything of what was lost.

It is from this spiritual essence that comes from the cosmic pre-birth world, the backbone of the now ripened "I"-consciousness, that spiritual forces and wisdom must grow. They will help form the future, not only of one particular life, but also the life of humanity in general. We can hardly understand how disturbing it is for the entire world that millions of children are losing their cosmic roots prematurely without our even knowing it.

The increase of criminality and general derailing of today's young people, which undoubtedly has many causes, is especially seen in those who lost their cosmic origins in early childhood. Punishment will not help. The first remedy that might heal this "sickness" of our time is to understand that the cosmic foundation has sunk *too deep*. What is needed is loving leadership that can subconsciously allow these soul foundations to rediscover the entrance to life: early childhood. It is the deeply sympathizing care of the young child that will heal this problem of our time. It is also this early, sound care that will allow adults to find the deeper meaning behind the road that leads upwards.

If a plant does not have healthy roots, its leaves and flowers will die, no matter how well it is cared for. The same is true for human beings. Proper care of our spiritual roots, in other words, letting our young children dream out their childhood dream and letting their cosmic content enter an earthly physical body, will be the beginning of the true ascent to further possibilities of human development.

We should never forget that everything we do for a child of any age works two ways—for the child, but also for the adult. This is true in a very special way with young children. With every experience, something of the cosmic content of the young child comes down to the earthly world, while the opposite happens for the adult. When we as adults connect with the cosmic essence of a young child, soul origins that have slumbered in us are touched and re-born. Each time this happens we take a small step "upwards," back to the cosmos, while the soul of the child takes small steps from its cosmic origin to the earthly world. For the adult, these small steps are taken with a new, slowly awakening *consciousness* and are actually steps forward. Through this newly acquired spiritual consciousness, we adults can rediscover our soul origins.

Thus the young child and the leading adult belong together. They form a natural soul or development unity. *We* lead the young child, but at the same time and without knowing it, we are led *by the child*. Each causes the other to take steps that both need.

We have seen what a blessing it is for the children if they can take their "steps" in a healthy way. What better way for group leaders to develop than through the care of these children? The task they have taken on, for the children and their parents, can also mean a deep schooling that completely fits each child's individual essence. Their work, which can be so fruitful for others, gives each leader the wonderful possibility to start a path of development in a unique way. There are few people who are given the opportunity to work so directly with human cosmic content.

As "outsiders" we cannot help but feel how quiet-yet-alive these developments are in the nursery and kindergarten groups, for both children and adults. What develops in this way will have a deep effect on the future, making the kindergarten groups essential for the development of humanity.

It is beautiful to see how the leaders of toddler and kindergarten groups are becoming more and more conscious of the meaning of their pressing task. No grandmother would have been able to guard these children against all the dangers of our time. It is the new toddler and kindergarten group leaders who are *conscious* of these dangers, are aware of the effect they have on young children, and can consciously protect them. Through this protection, the children will be able to develop in a safe and healthy way so that in later life their soul content can fulfill its task. Rudolf Steiner called doctors, spiritual leaders, and teachers a threesome who must work together for the future of humanity. Toddler and kindergarten leaders are not "teachers," but as "child leaders" they certainly belong to the third group and are therefore part of the threesome. Their task is to care for the children who still live in two worlds and who must be guided to deliver their cosmic content to the earthly world.

Spiritual science discusses at length how, through inner schooling, entrance to the spiritual world, the "upward ascent," can be achieved during earthly life. Children who have been able to "descend" to the earthly world while at least partly preserving their cosmic soul life will have created a foundation for this development.

But there is something else of importance. When returning "upwards" and crossing the threshold during life through spiritual schooling, nothing that is unripe or impermissible must pass. Ideally, the cosmic soul content of the children must "descend" *as completely as possible* and should be conscious within the helping adult. Unfortunately, this ideal is almost completely unattainable. Nevertheless the threshold must be crossed, with all the negative consequences that will follow. Thus it becomes even more evident how important it is that toddler and kindergarten leaders also keep watch over the soul content of the children as they make their way into this world. Only then can this content be a seed that can grow in later, adult life.

As discussed at the beginning of this chapter, the intimate toddler and kindergarten existence was in the past much closer to the old grandmother than to the mother. Due to her age, she had much more of the "threshold character" than anyone else in the family. It was the grandmother who cherished the little ones with her tenderness, giving them lap games, fairy tales, and so many other wonderful possibilities.

Nowadays this role must find new forms, usually fulfilled by very young leaders. Many of these will undoubtedly have the old grandmother's instinctive, warm affection in mind. If they can permeate this instinct with a consciousness for the hidden, unique qualities of the children, they will be able to give the children the fruitful leadership needed in our time. The most important thing is to try to consciously understand the leitmotif of early childhood: the gaining of confidence in this world while the soul still retains its cosmic life. Today this phenomenon must be led with understanding love in order not to be spoiled or ruined.

We can already do a great deal by trying to live with the children while they experience little "wonders" in everyday life. It is through these experiences that the cosmic soul content slowly creates a bond with the earthly world. Through our understanding compassion we will be able to create the most favorable surroundings for the children of our time.

When looking at these joyful but serious tasks, it might help to also look at the immense steps that the children have already taken in their soul life. After the long, gradual preparations for earthly life during life in the spiritual world, which was slowly closed off during the stay in the womb, physical birth is an abrupt change. Through its abrupt and strongly physical character, this change must be shocking for infants. One moment their small bodies are warm and protected, the next they are in the cold, unprotected, outside world. It will be obvious that their still-cosmic soul life must also experience an extreme shock. No wonder almost every child comes into this world crying, and *must* come crying in order to start its breathing life. On the other hand, it may be striking that many people leave this life with a smile on their face.

But birth is not a shocking experience only for the child. For the mother it comes with extreme pain, that often awakens her motherly love and allows it to come forward that much stronger.

For children the earthly surroundings are still so strange and different from their cosmic origins that their souls can find only a very small entrance to this new existence. The largest part of their essence must stay behind and will awaken slowly, searchingly, through the years, especially in childhood. In the infant years this mostly happens through the motherly love that the children receive, through which they recognize being carried and supported by higher beings.

In the toddler and kindergarten years, the more outward "remembrance experiences" come forward. This is the previously discussed "life in two worlds" in which children subconsciously meet something of cosmic content in earthly existence, and through which they slowly find entrance to this life.

According to legend, Gilgamesh of Babylon was two-thirds divine and one-third human. In other words, King Gilgamesh's soul, which was filled with the spirit, lingered for the most part in the spiritual world from which it received inspiration. Like Gilgamesh, the young child lives in two worlds at the same time, being carried by cosmic forces and receiving impulses from cosmic origins.

However, a difference is that young children must look for and get to know the earthly world. During this process, which mostly happens in dreaming "remembrance experiences," the group leaders must meet and help them *in their own way*. In order to help the children, the leaders must intimately understand what each child asks of them. We believe that the leaders are not alone in this task. They are helped by higher beings: the angels of each child. The angels stand at the threshold of heaven and send off the descending souls. The group leaders stand at the threshold of the earthly world and receive the children in order to accompany them into this world. The angel helps the soul to carry as many heavenly gifts with it as possible. Through understanding and warmth, the human helpers, the group leaders, bring the children the earthly knowledge they need to join their cosmic content and thus let it become part of their earthly life. Both toddler and kindergarten leaders stand ready to receive the children from their angels and lead them into this life in such a way that their cosmic essence and seeds are preserved. Thus, after physical birth and much physical care, this loving reception of the soul on the earthly side of the heavenly threshold is now their unique task: they are the "grandmothers" of our time.

People can encounter many different thresholds during a lifetime, but there is no one who helps others cross a threshold the way these early childhood helpers do. The hidden soul content that they help guide into this world, protecting it from too much damage, forms the foundation on which other educators can build. In adulthood, the individuals who have been guided in this way can consciously, of their own free will, develop the spiritual content that they brought with them. And in some cases, this development may bring something new and good to humanity.

Aside from the personal warmth of the leader, the atmosphere and character of the group as a whole is also important for the children as they experience crossing the threshold. Aside from the care of each individual child, this is another point to which the group leaders must devote attention. They will certainly be able to do this if they wholeheartedly live with the children in their passage across the threshold. Through compassion and insight, they will be able to change a group of children from a "pseudo family" into a healthy group of children: a new "family group." Thus all kinds of "new families" are born, where the children can be guarded from the negative influences of modern life, and find surroundings in which their cosmic seeds can sprout.

Finally, these new "families," where the essence of young children of various ages is truly understood, will undoubtedly contribute to the further development of humanity. Isn't what we expect from these children, who bring pre-birth content into this life, the active ingredient for ascension from our present depths? Through their love, care, and striving toward a true understanding of the young child, the leaders of toddler and kindergarten groups can lay a deep foundation for all humanity.

Music for the singing games

As this book is not primarily about singing games themselves but about the question of what the child can experience through them, the reader will only find a few examples. We have focused on the evolution these games have made from being played by school children on their own, to being led by adults in the kindergarten group.

The English translations of the songs sometimes depart from a strictly literal interpretation in order to preserve elements of sound and rhythm. Given the importance of these elements for the young child (see Chapter Six), this seemed a necessary sacrifice. The original Dutch lyrics are here included with each song for comparison. A few songs were omitted entirely because their meaning was tied to specific Dutch sounds or dialect words and was not translatable.

The songs are given in the order in which they appear in the text. For further discussion and explanation of the singing games, see the page reference after each song title.

I must wander (see page 46)

I must wan-der, must wan-der,___ O-ver hill and un-der. Here comes a mer-ry lit-tle jump-ing jack, He's wav-ing with his hat, He's stamp-ing with his foot! Come let us jump and dance, and dance, jump and dance, but the o-thers they must stay and stand.

Dutch: 'k Moet dwalen, 'k moet dwalen,
Langs bergen en langs dalen…
Daar komt een kleine springer in het veld!
Zwaaien met de hoed, stampen met de voet!
Kom wij willen springen gaan, dansen gaan
De anderen moeten blijven staan!

Note: Please change the pronouns according to the child who is playing.

Lay my hankie down (see page 54)

Dutch: *Zakdoekje leggen – niemand zeggen,*
'k Heb de hele nacht gewaakt,
Twee paar schoenen heb ik afgemaakt,
Eén van stof en één van leer,
Hier leg ik mijn zakdoekje neer.
Kijk voor je,
Kijk after je,
Aan allebei de zijden.

Note: In the text on page 54, this song is broken off after the fifth line without explanation. The entire song is included here for readers to use if and as they wish.

The seven leap (see page 57)

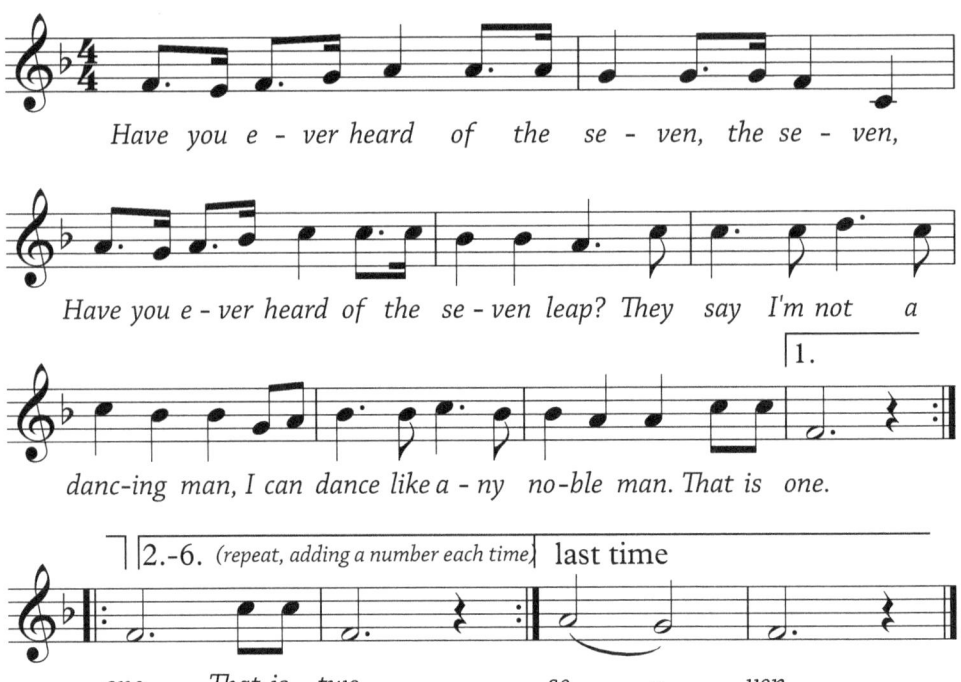

Dutch: *Heb je wel gehoord van de zeven, de zeven,*
Heb je wel gehoord van de zevensprong?
Ze zeggen dat ik niet dansen kan,
Ik kan dansen als een edelman!
Dat is één... dat is twee...

A pretty little mirror I have found (see page 60)

Dutch: *Ik heb een mooi mooi spiegeltje gevonden,*
Ik heb het op mijn hartje (om mijn halsje) gebonden,
Keer omme, keer omme,
En wie keert zich daar omme?
Mooi Rietje (Ons Keesje) heeft zich omme gekeerd,
Dat heeft zij (hij) van een lief meisje (van een jongetje) geleerd,
Keer omme, keer omme,
En Rietje (Keesje) keerde zich omme!

Note: Please change the pronouns and names according to the child who is playing.

Flowers blue in meadows green (see page 63)

Flow-ers blue in mead-ows green, Love-ly as the sil-ver's sheen,
Flowers in gar-lands wound, One dame must skip and bound. One
dame must still and si-lent stand, Then three times round is
our com-mand. And the dame she must kneel be-fore a friend to
start the game all o-ver a-gain. That will be,
that will be, that will be our (insert child's name).

Dutch: *Blauwe bloemen in het veld,*
't Is zo mooi als zilvergeld,
Blauwe bloemenkransen
En de jonkvrouw (jonker) die moet dansen
En de jonkvrouw (jonker) die moet stille staan,
Drie maal in de rondte gaan,
En de jonkvrouw (jonker) die moet knielen
En weer een andere kiezen,
Dat zal zijn, dat zal zijn,
Dat zal onze Liesje (Johan) zijn.

Note: Please sing "dame" or "gent" according to the child who is playing.

Fair Anna (see page 65)

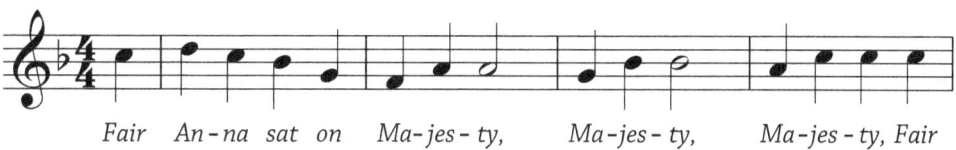

Fair An-na sat on Ma-jes-ty, Ma-jes-ty, Ma-jes-ty, Fair An-na sat on Ma-jes-ty, Ma-jes-ty.

And then her dear old Mother came...
Say, Anna, why are you weeping so?...
I weep because I have to die...
Why do you have to go and die?...
That wicked Frederick, he did that!...
He has just gone and made her dead...
Now she's been put into a box...
But look, she stands up happily...
Now she becomes an angel pure...
The angel chooses another child...

Dutch: *Mooi Anna zat op Majesteit, majesteit, majesteit,*
Mooi Anna zat op Majesteit, ma-jes-teit.
Daar kwam haar lieve Moeder aan, Moeder aan, Moeder aan...
Zeg Anna waarom ween je zo?...
Ik ween omdat ik sterven moet...
Wat zal jij moeten sterven gaan?...
Dat doet die boze Fre-de-rik!...
Die heeft haar zo maar dood gedaan...
Nu wordt zij in een kistje gelegd...
Maar zie, zij staat weer vrolijk op...
Zo wordt zij nu een engel rein...
De engel kiest weer 'n mensenkind...

We come from far-off lands (see page 69)

What have you brought for us? Margo... *(repeat refrain with each verse)*
A basket of golden roses...
For whom will those then be?...
They're for my dearest one...
And who's your dearest one?...

Ending:

Note: Because no clear way of putting this final verse together with the tune was given, we have taken the liberty of creating this version. The actual child's name should be inserted, and can be repeated in place of the "Margo, Margo, Margogely" refrain if desired.

Dutch: *Wij komen uit verre landen,*
Margo, Margo, Margocheltje,
Wij komen uit verre landen,
Margocheltje.

Wat heb je voor ons meegebracht? Margo...
Een mandje met gouden rozen. Margo...
Voor wie zal dat wel wezen? Margo...
't Is voor mijn allerliefste, Margo...
Wie is je allerliefste? Margo...
Dat zal zijn, dat zal zijn, dat zal onze (Dora, Pieter) zijn.

We're the poor Marionsen (see page 72)

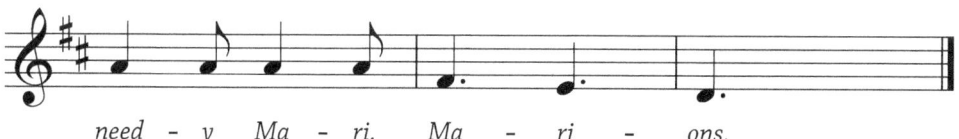

We're the rich and wealthy, wealthy, Marionsen, Marionetten... (repeat refrain)
I would like to wed your daughter...
I don't have one you can marry...
I had heard that you do have one...
She is not for you to marry...
I shall give her pretty clothing...
It's not enough for you to marry...
Then I'll kneel right down before her (or Then I will give her heaven)...
Well then you can go and wed her...

Dutch: *Wij zijn arme, arme, arme Marionsen, Marionetten,*
Wij zijn arme, arme, arme Mari – Marions!

Wij zijn rijke, rijke, rijke Marionsen...
'k Wou zo graag uw dochter trouwen, Marionsen...
' Heb er geen om mee te trouwen, Marionsen...
'k Heb gehoord, dat gij er een hadt, Marionsen...
Die is niet om mee te trouwen, Marionsen...
'k Zal haar (mooie kleren) geven, Marionsen...
Daarvoor kunt ge haar niet trouwen, Marionsen...
Dan zal 'k voor haar nederknielen, Marionsen...
óf: Dan zal 'k haar de hemel geven, Marionsen...
Daarvoor kun je haar wel trouwen, Marionsen...

I would make a string of beads (see page 77)

I would make a string of beads, but I lack the thread I need,

Ha, ha, vic-to-ri-a, Ha, ha, vic-to-ri-a!

Dutch: *'k Wou zo graag een ketting rijgen*
Maar ik kon de draad niet krijgen
Ha, ha, victoria,
Ha, ha, victoria!

Between France and Germany (see page 81)

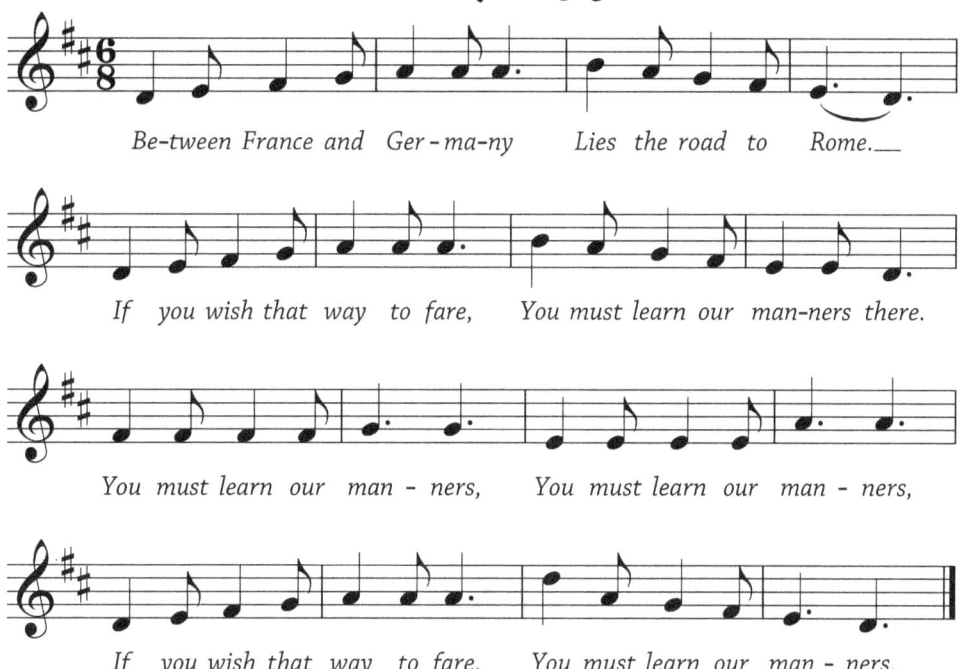

Be-tween France and Ger-ma-ny Lies the road to Rome.
If you wish that way to fare, You must learn our man-ners there.
You must learn our man-ners, You must learn our man-ners,
If you wish that way to fare, You must learn our man-ners.

Dutch: *Tussen Keulen en Parijs*
Ligt de weg naar Rome.
Al wie met ons mee wil gaan
Die moet onze manieren verstaan.
Zo zijn onze manieren,
Zo zijn onze manieren,
Zo zijn onze manieren, manieren,
Zo zijn onze manieren.

White swans and black swans (see page 86)

White swans and black swans, Who will sail with us to Eng - land?

Eng-land is locked up tight,___ The key is bro-ken quite.___

Is there no smith in the land Who can help with his strong hand? Come

forth now, Come forth now, The last one shall come forth now.

Dutch: *Witte zwanen, zwarte zwanen,*
Wie gaat er mee naar Engeland varen?
Engeland is gesloten,
De sleutel is gebroken.
Is er dan geen smit in het land,
Die onze sleutel maken kan?
Laat doorgaan, laat doorgaan
Wie achter is komt vooraan.
Of
De laatste wordt gevangen.

The Watchman (see page 90)

Dutch: *Zeg Klepperman van elleven*
Waarheen ga jij zo laat?
Langs alle slapende kinderen,
Daar waar de wind heen gaat. (Fine)
En mijn klepper gaat van klap, klap, klap,
En mijn voeten gaan van stap, stap, stap! (D.C. al Fine)

Shoe the horse now (see page 91)

Shoe the horse now! Who'll do it and how? John, the smith, so well can he do, Up-on each hoof he'll put the shoe! Clop, clop, clop-pit-y clop, And the hor-sie goes hop, hop, hop, hop! Hop hop, hop hop, hop hop, hop.

Dutch: *Peerdje beslaan! Wie heeft dat gedaan?*
Jan de smed, die kan dat zo net,
Die heeft er het ijzerke ondergezet!
Klop, klop, kloppedy, klop.

I am a blacksmith good and true (see page 99)

I am a black-smith good and true, Best of work I al-ways do. All day

long my ham-mers go, Cling-ing, cling-ing, clang-ing so. A rick-e-ty

dick-e-ty dick-e-ty dick, A rick-e-ty dick-e-ty dick-e-ty dick.

Dutch: *Ben ik dan niet een flinke smid,*
Die met vlijt de kost moet winnen?
Dat gaat zo maar altijd voort,
Alle dagen zoals het behoort.
Van rikkerde tikkerde tikkerde tik! (bis)

Note: This English version is reproduced by permission from *Let Us Form a Ring* (Acorn Hill Waldorf Kindergarten and Nursery), page 2.

The Washerwomen (see page 100)

Dutch: *Laat zien uwe voeten, laat zien uwe schoen;*
Laat zien, wat die vlijtige wasvrouwen doen!
Zij wassen, zij wassen, zij wassen de hele dag! (bis)
Zij wringen...
Zij hangen...
Zij strijken...
Zij drinken... een kopje thee
Zij eten... een lekk're koek
Zij kletsen...
Zij dansen...
Zij slapen...

Note: English words adapted by permission from *Merrily We Sing* by Ilian Willwerth (WECAN, 2014), page 21—please see this version for a melody in the mood of the fifth.

Notes

1 Rudolf Steiner, *The Education of the Child and Early Lectures on Education* (Anthroposophic Press, 1996).

2 See Rudolf Steiner, *The Education of the Child (op. cit.).*

3 See *The Mood of the Fifth: A Musical Approach to Early Childhood*, edited by Nancy Foster (WECAN, 2013).

4 See Rudolf Steiner, *An Outline of Esoteric Science* (Anthroposophic Press, 1997) and *Theosophy* (Anthroposophic Press, 1994).

5 See also Franz E. Winkler, *Man, the Bridge Between Two Worlds* (Harper, 1960).

6 Author's note: This question will be partly answered in the next chapter and in Chapter Six in the part on line games.

7 Translation note: In Dutch, the specific sounds of the verbs in different tenses have a significance which is lost in translation, and so they are not discussed here. The phrase "Springer in het veld" can't really be translated— it is a jumping jack, young colt, madcap, comedian, joker, prankster—all in a childlike, positive sense.

8 Author's note: Walking or wandering and singing around the circle *alone* can force the youngest children to wake up. In order to prevent this we can assign an older child to accompany him and then all join in at the words "Here comes. . ." Sometimes it will be better to sing the whole song together.

9 Author's note: The background of a certain motif in a fairy tale or game cannot be "explained." We are asked to listen closely to what it wants to communicate to us subconsciously, not what we decide the explanation should be. When listening in this way, we will see that one motif will have many different experiences. A word will mean one thing in one language and something completely different in another. In much the same way, the "words" in the "language" of images can be varied. Thus we will have to try to follow the images that fairy tales or games create. For example, we can feel something for the child walking outside the circle who is trying to find entrance into the human circle, while the other children feel a strong bonding Fatherly element, both with the same motif.

10 Author's note: Through the rather illogical words it will be even clearer that the content of this song is not about logic. It is the image content that speaks to us through the game form, movements, melody, and rhythmic drama, and also through a few of the words. It is the goal of this book to find a way to the more hidden experiences of young children by way of our logic and feeling, in order to not only be able to lead the singing games more effectively but also to come closer to the children themselves.

11 See Rudolf Steiner, *An Outline of Esoteric Science*.

12 See Bernard Lievegoed, *Maat – Rithme – Melodie* (W. de Haan, 1939). "Beat – Rhythm – Melody," not available in English.

13 Translation note: We have not attempted to translate the refrain, which we may enjoy for its repeated sounds and rhythmical quality without being overly concerned with the literal meaning of the words. "Marionetten" signifies "marionettes," puppets operated from above by strings, which in turn is derived from French, "Little Mary" (referring to puppets of the Virgin Mary). The nonsense words "Mari," "Marions," "Marionsen" are apparently simply variations on this theme.

14 Translation note: Unfortuately, at this point the author refers to another Dutch book for the exact instructions as to how to play this game. We were unable to locate the book, but assume that the game is very similar to the one previously discussed.

15 Translation note: The original text reads "must then naturally be played by a boy kneeling in front of a girl." Today we may find this quite old-fashioned, and might choose not to have gender play a role even in this line of the game.

16 Author's note: In hidden and overt ways, both fairy tales and singing games show a connection between the human soul and its earthly life. It is interesting to note that human morals play no role here. This is appropriate since children in the kindergarten years are not ready for morals. Of course, quick looks or light reprimands can be given as a guide. Expecting deeper moral behavior from a kindergartner is impossible, as this is not understood by a child of this age. We should wait to expect this behavior until a child is seven to eight years old when, helped by his imagination, he has more understanding of himself and his surroundings. Fables, which show morals in a humorous and imaginative way, are then useful.

17 Author's note: Eurythmically speaking, isn't forcing these little ones to create the excessively strong E-form with their arms worrying as well?

18 Translation note: The original Dutch refers to the cities of Paris and Cologne. The country names have been substituted as they are more suitable to the rhythm of the song, as well as perhaps more familiar to American and other English-speaking children.

19 Author's note: In a lecture about the stained glass windows of the first Goetheanum, Mr D.J. van Bemmelen spoke about the spiritual meaning of the "Columns of Hercules," between which one sailed to the "ocean of the soul." It would not be surprising if the beacons in this game, between which the soul must find its way to the spiritual ideal "Rome," are the Christian counterpart to the "Columns of Hercules."

20 Author's note: At this point we should also remember the "Mirror" game and "Flowers blue" (both circle games) and the back-and-forth game "We come from far-off lands."

21 Author's note: For us this is quite different than for young children. In the relationship between the cosmic and earthly world, the children can more easily be compared to people of ancient humanity, who were also still connected to their cosmic origins. In early childhood the "key to England (Angel-land)" has not been completely broken. In addition, young children are more focused on the earthly world that will give them their desired future. As we see in many fairy tales and singing games, the children experience the images from "two worlds" that lead them to *earth* rather than back to the cosmos. This early childhood experience gives us as adults the chance to use these same images for *our* future: to rediscover the spiritual world. We should remember this unusual relationship when looking at this game.

22 Author's note: One could think about the return to the spiritual world when crossing the threshold of death (as discussed in the games "I must wander" and "Lay my hankie down"): excarnation at the end of life. But, in this case, this cannot be what is "meant," even though human beings can *prepare* for death but do not have to forge the key to death's door, i.e. death itself. Forging this key clearly points towards completion of the inner schooling that must be accomplished during and for this life.

23 Author's note: Compare the inner "about-turn of the soul" in the "Mirror" game.

24 Author's note: See the discussion of the "String of beads" game.

25 Author's note: Compare the "poor of soul" also to the "stupid younger brother" and "sister" in fairy tales; see Chapter Eight.

26 Translation note: In Dutch, "Klepperman" is the name of the watchman and "klepper" his warning rattle.

27 Author's note: This is also the reason that we will not discuss the arts. There is no clear boundary between the arts and work, but the arts search for the way from the earth to the spirit while the child searches for the way from the spirit to the earth. Children also do this when painting, drawing, or playing with clay. This is why the arts, as we see them as adults, lie in their future.

28 Author's note: See Chapter Nine for the possible mystery origins of the old folk games. The oldest games portraying crafts can hardly be seen as the craft games of today. Think about the "Watchman" game, which in its oldest form (substituted in this book by a newer variation) did not really portray the work. These games originated in a time when adults also still lived in a more or less dreaming state of consciousness and thus experienced their work as joyful "dream-games." How could people of that time feel the need to make a realistic game out of their work? Nowadays, artists who sculpt, paint or conduct would not do so either.

29 Author's note: Using the official numbering system for the Grimms' tales, this brief story is found in KHM 105, "Märchen von der Unke." In the Netherlands there is a well-known translation by M.M. de Vries-Vogel in which the toad is replaced by a "house snake," and in English, too, a common translation to be found is called "Stories about Snakes." This has caused the content of the fairy tale to be changed completely and lose its original meaning. It is not for nothing that the snake, a reptile that slides over the earth, seduced mankind (mythologically) and caused the Fall, or in other words caused mankind to also "glide low to the ground." Neither in their form, nor in the way they live so close to the ground, do snakes have any parallel to the life-in-two-worlds of the small child. In contrast, frogs and toads, as amphibians, *do*. However, let's not confuse this with the Grimm fairy tale "The White Snake" in which the image of the snake, especially in its white disguise, is completely correct!

30 Author's note: A healthy newcomer, when asked to participate in singing games, will usually refuse. I have even heard of a case where a child was shocked and started to cry. We should try to understand and feel for the children if they react in this way. These newcomers, especially the younger ones, some of whom are very sensitive, can feel an almost frightening alienation from the world of singing games, a world that they are not yet ready for and in which they could lose themselves if they were to participate at too early an age. These children should therefore be given an extra long and peaceful acclimation period.

31 Author's note: Procrustes had a bed in which he let everyone sleep but then stretched or shortened the limbs to "fit" the bed.

32 Author's note: Children who slowly awaken are not always the youngest in the family. The "youngest" in fairy tales can therefore be seen as an expression for those who act out of their true, deeper "I." The "I" is that part of a human being that incarnates last and is therefore the youngest and the least developed, although oldest in meaning. It is at the same time the "youngest" and "dumbest," but still the most important of the "brothers" that together make up our being.

33 Author's note: See the games "We are the poor Marionsen" and "White swans and black swans" in Chapter Seven.

34 Author's note: In the fairy tale, Cinderella is not the youngest but the stepsister who is seen as the "least" by the others. This does not matter in this context. In some fairy tales, for example "Mother Holle," there are two sisters one of whom is the stepsister.

35 Author's note: Other fairy tales to be considered are "The Golden Goose," "The Griffin," "The Hut in the Forest" (all by Grimm) and many other fairy tales from Norway, Russia, and other countries.

36 Author's note: A new danger that threatens singing games and young children is that people use this cultural heritage as a kind of orientation in traffic, in other words an awakening with regard to traffic in the streets. After everything we have said, it will be understood what fatal consequences such an awakening, also on this level, will have for the games themselves and especially for the children. It is sacrilege of a profoundly spiritual matter. It is obvious that we need to look for more safety for young children with regards to traffic. This is a task for all adults and should certainly not be given to the children themselves. M.L. van Goudoever once suggested, "Why shouldn't we create a traffic draft, much like the military draft for young men, for young unmarried women and girls geared towards leading toddlers and kindergartners through traffic?"

37 Rudolf Steiner, *Karmic Relationships, Volume III,* lecture of July 13, 1924.

38 Translation note: This section refers to the time of this book's original publication in the late twentieth century.

39 Author's note: On the structure of the Mass and its renewal in The Act of Consecration of Man, see *The Eucharist* by Rudolf Frieling (available as a free PDF download at florisbooks.co.uk). See also Chapters Six and Seven on back-and-forth games.

40 Author's note: Dr. T. Jurriaanse spoke about this story during a lecture in Zeist, the Netherlands. See Wilhelm Michaelis, *Die apokryphen Schriften zum neuen Testament* (Anaconda Verlag, 2013). "The Apocryphal Writings on the New Testament," not available in English.

41 Rudolf Steiner, *Michaelmas and the Soul Forces of Man* (Anthroposophic Press, 1982), lecture of September 27, 1923.

42 Author's note: In its first form as spoken by Rudolf Steiner on December 25, 1923 in the Schreinerei by the new Goetheanum.

43 Rudolf Steiner, *The Cycle of the Year as Breathing Process of the Earth* (Anthroposophic Press, 1984), lecture of April 7, 1923.

44 Author's note: Singing to St. Nicholas by the fireplace can be traced back to the worship of Odin through the smoke duct in the roof in Germanic times. The fires that burned in some regions during Christian festivities (Easter, Whitsun, Feast of John) must date back to heathen times when mankind used fire and smoke to worship their gods.

Recommended resources

Daniel Udo de Haes's earlier work, *The Creative Word: The Young Child's Experience of Language and Stories* (WECAN, 2014) is essential reading in conjunction with the present volume, in order to fill out the picture of the young child's developing consciousness. It specifically addresses the transformation that takes place between toddlerhood and kindergarten age.

By the same author, *Kleuterwereld-Sprookjeswereld* ("The world of the kindergartner—The world of fairy tales") is also highly recommended for its insights into the consciousness of the young child in relation to fairy tales; this book has not yet been translated into English.

Works by Rudolf Steiner

The Education of the Child and Early Lectures on Education (Anthroposophic Press, 1996) is an important summary of basic anthroposophical ideas related to pedagogy and child development.

The Spiritual Guidance of the Individual and Humanity (Anthroposophic Press, 1991), is another fundamental work that sheds light on child development in the early years. See particularly Lecture One.

An Outline of Esoteric Science (Anthroposophic Press, 1997) and *Theosophy* (Anthroposophic Press, 1994) present Steiner's view of the human being as an entity of body, soul, and spirit, and of humanity's place within an evolving cosmos that has its origin in spiritual processes and beings.

The Cycle of the Year as Breathing Process of the Earth (Anthroposophic Press, 1984) reveals the deep relationship between humanity, the earth, and the cycle of the seasons, and demonstrates how the seasonal festivals can illuminate and strengthen humanity's connection to the Christ Being.

Pentatonic and mood-of-the-fifth music

The Mood of the Fifth: A Musical Approach to Early Childhood, edited by Nancy Foster (WECAN, 2013) is a thorough exploration of the "mood of the fifth," the form of pentatonic music that Rudolf Steiner suggested as most suitable for the consciousness of the young child, and of the experience of music in early childhood in general.

A Day Full of Song: Work Songs from a Waldorf Kindergarten by Karen Lonsky (WECAN, 2009) and *Merrily We Sing: Original Songs in the Mood of the Fifth* by Ilian Willwerth (WECAN, 2014) contain songs in the mood of the fifth for many occasions and events of the kindergarten, including some singing games.

Pentatonic Songs: For Nursery, Kindergarten, Grades One and Two by Elisabeth Lebret (Waldorf School Association of Ontario, 1985) is a classic resource for pentatonic music appropriate for young children.

Other songs and singing games

Let Us Form a Ring and *Dancing As We Sing* (Acorn Hill Waldorf Kindergarten and Nursery, distributed by WECAN) are two much-loved collections of songs, games, and circles for nursery and kindergarten groups.

Kinderzang en kinderspel ("Child's song and child's play," two volumes, not available in English) by Kes, Pollman and Tiggers contains many of the songs included in this book as well as dozens more from the Dutch tradition.

About the author

Daniel Udo de Haes was born in 1899 into a family with six children in Bali, Indonesia (then under Dutch colonial rule). In his ninth year, the family moved to Holland. Daniel studied physics and mathematics at Leiden University and became a teacher in the Hague. He then went to Zeist and encountered the Anthroposophy of Rudolf Steiner, which inspired all his further work.

At a conference he met his future wife, Johanna van Goudover, with whom he had three children. In Zeist, he taught in a Waldorf elementary school, and then worked until his retirement as a teacher in an anthroposophic institute for children with special needs, "Het Zonnehuis."

Toward the end of this period he wrote, illustrated, and self-published a series of books for young children, *Zonnegeheimen*, containing tales, fables and small poems. After his retirement he also wrote a series of educational books for parents and teachers. A focus of his work was the importance of telling the traditional fairy tales to young children. He continued with these educational writings up to his death in March, 1986, in Zeist.

Other WECAN books you will enjoy:

The Creative Word
The Young Child's Experience of Language and Stories
Daniel Udo de Haes

A fascinating exploration of the consciousness of very young children, and of how we can best support their development through language. **$16**

Let Us Form a Ring
Dancing As We Sing
The Acorn Hill Anthologies
Edited by Nancy Foster

Two classic collections of songs, singing games, and circles for nursery and kindergarten groups. Learning CDs are also available. **$20 per volume**

The Mood of the Fifth
A Musical Approach to Early Childhood
Edited by Nancy Foster

A resource for understanding and working with music in the mood of the fifth, so important in supporting the healthy development of young children from birth through the age of nine. **$20**

845-352-1690 • information@waldorfearlychildhood.org
store.waldorfearlychildhood.org

Other WECAN books you will enjoy:

Tell Me a Story
Stories from the Waldorf Early Childhood Association of North America
Edited by Louise deForest

Contributed by members and friends of WECAN, over 80 of our favorite stories for all ages and all occasions. **$25**

The Wilma Ellersiek Gesture Games Series:
Giving Love—Bringing Joy
Gesture Games for Spring and Summer
Gesture Games for Autumn and Winter
Dancing Hand—Trotting Pony

A bounteous feast of life-giving song, movement and gesture. **Each volume $28**

A Lifetime of Joy
A Collection of Circle Games, Finger Games, Songs, Verses and Plays
Bronja Zahlingen

A treasure trove of nourishment is found in this collection that Bronja gathered over many years of work with children and the adults who care for them. **$18**

845-352-1690 • information@waldorfearlychildhood.org
store.waldorfearlychildhood.org